HIKING TRAILS 3
Northern Vancouver Island

Great Central Lake to Cape Scott featuring
Strathcona Park plus Malcolm, Quadra, Nootka,
Hornby Islands and new trails everywhere

Revised and expanded by Gil Parker

TENTH EDITION, 2008

VANCOUVER ISLAND TRAILS
INFORMATION SOCIETY (VITIS)

Tenth edition copyright © 2008
Vancouver Island Trails Information
Society

Original copyright © 1975; Outdoor
Club of Victoria Trails Information
Society. Revised and/or reprinted 1977,
1979, 1982, 1986, 1990, 1992, 1994,
1996, 2002. Society name change, 1993,
to Vancouver Island Trails Information
Society.

Illustrations
John S.T. Gibson, Judy Trousdell

Cover photo
Douglas Cowell

Photos
Credit for each photo is shown
with photo

Book design
Frances Hunter, Beacon Hill
Communications Group Inc.

Map production and revisions
Jim Bisakowski, Desktop Publishing Ltd.

**National Library of Canada Cataloguing
in Publication**

Hiking Trails 3/Gil Parker, editor. — 10th ed.
(Hiking Trails of Vancouver Island; 3)
Previous eds. published under title: Hiking
Trails III. Includes bibliographical references
and index.

ISBN 978-0-9697667-6-6

1. Trails—British Columbia—Vancouver
Island—Guidebooks. 2. Hiking—British
Columbia—Vancouver Island—Guidebooks.
3. Vancouver Island (B.C.)—Guidebooks.
I. Parker, Gil II. Vancouver Island Trails
Information Society III. Series. IV. Title:
Hiking Trails 3.

GV199.44. C22V352008a 796.5109711'2
C2008-903740-5

*Printed and bound in Canada by Friesens, Altona,
Manitoba. Distributed by Orca Book Publishers,
Victoria, BC*

ENVIRONMENTAL BENEFITS STATEMENT

Vancouver Island Trails Information Society saved
the following resources by printing the pages of
this book on chlorine free paper made with
100% post-consumer waste.

TREES	WATER	ENERGY	SOLID WASTE	GREENHOUSE GASES
61	22,230	42	2,855	5,356
FULLY GROWN	GALLONS	MILLION BTUs	POUNDS	POUNDS

Calculations based on research by Environmental Defense and
the Paper Task Force. Manufactured at Friesens Corporation.

Vancouver Island Trails Information Society (VITIS)

web page: www.hikingtrailsbooks.com
e-mail: trails@hikingtrailsbooks.com
telephone: Victoria area 250-474-5043

toll free: 1-866-598-0003
fax: Victoria area 250-474-4577
toll free fax: 1-888-258-4213

It is necessary that all persons take responsibility for their own actions. The
Vancouver Island Trails Information Society and the Editor will not be held
liable for any mishap occurring as a consequence of any misunderstanding or
misrepresentation of any content of this book or for any errors or omissions.
Each hiker is responsible for his/her own safety. While every effort is made
to ensure the accuracy of the hike descriptions and correctness of the advice,
hikers must take all reasonable care to ensure that when a hike is undertaken
they will be able to do the hike safely. See also the Hints and Cautions Section
of the book.

Contents

Hikers on trail to Castlecrag, Paradise Meadows. GIL PARKER

General Map of Northern Vancouver Island

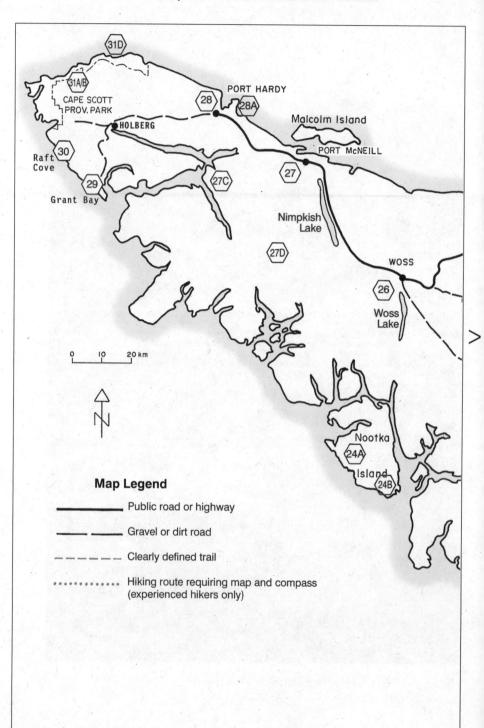

Map Legend

—————— Public road or highway

— — — — Gravel or dirt road

- - - - - - Clearly defined trail

·············· Hiking route requiring map and compass
(experienced hikers only)

General Map of Northern Vancouver Island

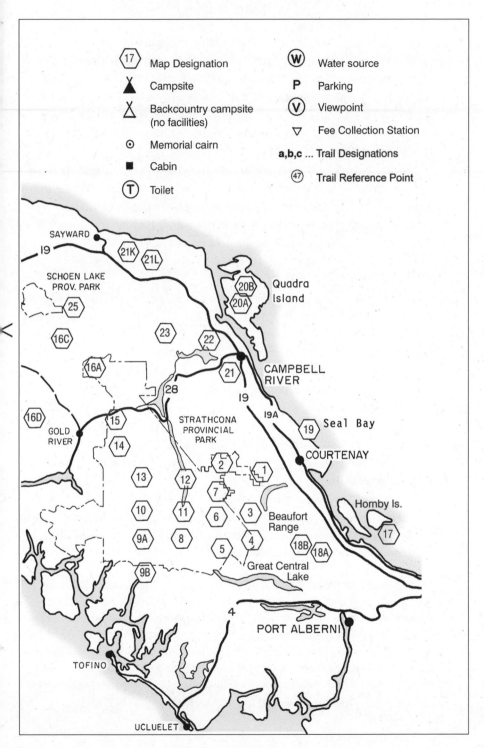

Legend:

- (17) Map Designation
- △ (filled tent) Campsite
- △ (open tent) Backcountry campsite (no facilities)
- ⊙ Memorial cairn
- ■ Cabin
- (T) Toilet
- (W) Water source
- P Parking
- (V) Viewpoint
- ▽ Fee Collection Station
- **a,b,c** ... Trail Designations
- (47) Trail Reference Point

SAYWARD

19

SCHOEN LAKE PROV. PARK

21K 21L

25

16C

23

20B
20A

Quadra Island

22

16A

28

21

CAMPBELL RIVER

19

16D

15

19A

Seal Bay

GOLD RIVER

14

STRATHCONA PROVINCIAL PARK

19

COURTENAY

13

2

1

12

7

Hornby Is.

10

11

6

3

Beaufort Range

9A

8

4

17

5

18B 18A

9B

Great Central Lake

4

PORT ALBERNI

TOFINO

UCLUELET

Map Notes

A contour line is simply all the points of the same elevation joined together. Where contour lines are close together it indicates that the terrain is steeper than where the lines are farther apart. This is most useful for determining where you are, as you can readily assess steepness, locate creeks and ridges, and calculate the effort that will be required. A contour (topographical) map and aerial photograph are useful adjuncts to the trail descriptions in this book.

Contour lines on our maps are at different intervals, mainly to suit the topographic maps that are currently being published. While many topographic maps are in metric with 40 m or 20 m contour lines, some—especially in the north Island—still contain elevations and contours in feet. Most topographic maps are based upon a scale of 1:50,000, but check each map for scale and contour interval. Conversions: 100 m = 328 ft; 40 m = 131.2 ft ; 20 m = 65.6 ft.

Maps currently sold for Vancouver Island are based on both North American Datums (both NAD27 and NAD83). If you are using GPS devices, you must know which system you are using. GPS grids noted herein show both NAD systems.

TRIM maps 1:20,000 are also reliable references. The Terrain Resource Information Management program is comprised of 7,027 map sheets covering the entire province of British Columbia. These maps are based on the Universal Transverse Mercator (UTM) coordinate system, depicted using the North American Datum 1983 (NAD83).

You should purchase your own maps because we have not reproduced all their information.

Every effort has been made to ensure accuracy in this book. If you find that there are discrepancies, for whatever reason, please inform VITIS at www.hikingtrailsbooks.com or Email to trails@hikingtrailsbooks.com. Hike updates are posted on this website.

Map Credits: Some maps are based on 1:50,000 (2cm = 1 km) National Topographical Series (NTS) maps, printed in grey and blue, with overlays for trails and other features. These maps have been reproduced with the permission of Natural Resources Canada 2008, courtesy of the Centre for Topographic Information: 92 F/5 Bedwell River, 92 F/6 Great Central Lake, 92 F/7 Horne Lake , 92 F/11 Forbidden Plateau, 92 F/12 Buttle Lake, 92 F/13 Upper Campbell Lake. Clover Point Cartographics: base maps for M21L, M21K, M27D. Strategic Forest Management supplied base map for M31D. Comox Strathcona R.D. supplied map for M17.

How To Use This Book

Users of previous editions of *Hiking Trails 3* will notice a major reorganization of the material. The appropriate map for each "Section" is located as close as possible to the trail descriptions for that map. Obviously, some trails or routes extend to other maps and where this occurs, reference page locations are given in the trail descriptions. Page locations for trail/route descriptions and the primary map associated with that Section are given in the "Contents."

Hiking Trails 3 describes trails and wilderness routes in some of the most beautiful areas of northern and central Vancouver Island. We make no attempt here to recommend the sort of equipment, clothing or food that a backcountry trip entails, as there are many books and guides available that do this, and other enthusiasts to offer you conflicting opinions. Preparing for a trip can be as much fun as the trip itself and we hope we are supplying tools to help you do your homework for route and trail conditions before setting out.

Hiking Trails 3 provides a key to the door, a portal beyond which you are on your own. It is essential that you read the text rather than simply try to follow the dashes and dots on our maps. The wilderness route descriptions are perhaps the most valuable part of this book, having been inspired by persons who have been there. Certain junctions have been pinpointed using GPS co-ordinates, confirmed in the field, for topographic maps.

Our text should be read in conjunction with our maps, and also the corresponding topographic maps. References to altitude and compass directions are frequently used to locate positions. Hiking times given are average group times as taken over the years by experienced parties, carrying packs.

In this book, a *trail* is a way that has been built by people or travelled regularly by animals so it is obvious. Trails are sometimes signed, marked with cairns or flagged with tape.

A *route* indicates a possible way to go, though on the ground there may be nothing to see, except the lay of the land as understood by an experienced hiker. Our maps show trails and routes and only experienced hikers or groups with very experienced leaders should attempt to follow wilderness routes.

In all cases, hikers must be self-reliant. Responsible hikers will have an experienced leader and will know how to use navigation devices to avoid becoming lost. These hikers will always carry the right maps, a good compass or GPS and an altimeter. They will also carry a first aid kit, overnight survival gear and be able to deal with emergencies.

In general, all description of trails and routes *apply to the summer months*, and sometimes there may be comments made about circumstances at other seasons. However, conditions in winter (and sometimes spring and early summer) are vastly different. Conditions of the terrain in these seasons should not be assumed to be the same as described for summer months.

Hints and Cautions

This guidebook deals with a wide variety of trails and routes. While all outdoor activity should be the result of careful planning and proper physical conditioning, hikers must choose activities appropriate to their skills and experience. The following cautions apply to all hiking and, while Strathcona Park contains remote wilderness and special regulations to maintain its particular resources, the same care and attention to the natural environment applies wherever you hike.

Strathcona Park is experiencing more use than ever, and some areas are literally being loved to death. BC Parks' staff has lessened user impact by building trails, designating camping areas, providing toilets and restricting the use of campfires.

The Park Master Plan, developed with a great deal of public input, designates most backcountry areas to "wilderness conservation." While this ensures that floatplanes and helicopters do not land there, this category does not permit BC Parks to do significant maintenance, provide any facilities, including toilets, or even place signs. In fact, these backcountry areas are solely dependent on their isolation for their continued preservation.

This means you alone bear the responsibility for how much you impact the region. Obviously, this can only work if all hikers passing through ensure they leave no lasting trace. A concern to preserve Strathcona Park's wilderness experience has led the hiking community to adopt the convention of not building cairns or flagging obvious routes (unless absolutely necessary due to washouts, blowdowns, avalanche debris or logging). Leaving such markers may lead others into areas beyond their competence.

BC Parks has provided pit toilets at various "front country" locations. Elsewhere, use the bush well away from streams. Carry a trowel so you can dig a small scat hole. Either bury toilet paper very well, burn it or pack it out in a plastic bag, because it will take a long time to decompose. An ice axe can also be a multi-use tool! There are several good guidebooks on outdoor sanitation practices and procedures. Take out all your garbage, and if you find some left by others, carry that out also.

In core areas BC Parks has restricted camping to specific, hardened sites and no fires are permitted. No campfires will be permitted in the backcountry of Strathcona Park; camp stoves are the essential alternative. Fires are permitted only at designated fire rings at high-use campgrounds (such as the Buttle Lake and Ralph River campsites on Buttle Lake) and various marine sites. In core areas and fee zones where specified, camp only on hardened sites.

Even in areas outside Strathcona Park, campfire activities such as wood collection, burn scars and incompletely burned garbage make campfires the single most damaging human impact on sensitive areas. Always practice low-impact camping.

Most of British Columbia's provincial forests are owned by the public and leased and managed by forest companies. Recreation (camping and picnicking) sites and trails, developed by the BC Forest Service (BCFS) and logging companies on provincial forestlands, are managed for multiple use. Most recreation facilities within provincial jurisdiction are now overseen by the Ministry of Tourism, Culture and the Arts.

Access information on logging roads may be obtained from timber company offices, or regional tourism offices. See Appendix. Ask locally for recreation and logging road guides. Due to problems with narrow roads, vandalism or fire hazard, access to logging roads is often limited. Roads may be "open", with travel permitted at all times; "restricted," with travel permitted only during non-working hours (normally from about 5:00 pm to 6:30 am and on week-ends and holidays); or "closed." Access restrictions may change frequently with little notice. Loggers sometimes work holidays and weekends. Roads are generally closed when fire hazard is high or are open only in the mornings, even when general BCFS closures are not in effect. A long distance call a day or two in advance of a trip is often a worthwhile investment. Obey posted signs. Some open gates may be locked later when you need to leave.

Always have your vehicle's headlights on when travelling logging roads. These dirt and gravel arteries can be extremely dusty. If you are sharing the road with industrial traffic and a logging truck is approaching, the safest procedure is to pull well over to the side of the road and wait until the oncoming traffic has passed. Trucks often travel in groups so do not be in a hurry to pull back onto the road after one has passed. Always yield to loaded trucks, particularly on narrow roads and when they are travelling downhill. This may mean backing rapidly to a turn-off.

Exercise special care in remote areas. Many regions in this book are out of reach of immediate help in emergencies and cell phones are unreliable in mountains and valleys. Most logging vehicles carry radios and there are telephones at logging camps.

Carry appropriate maps, a compass, altimeter and/or GPS. A GPS is not a substitute for a map and compass. Even on a trail you can easily lose your way, especially in fog. Although trails are generally well marked, they tend to become hard to follow or even obliterated in places by slides, periodic flooding or tree blowdowns.

Always leave a trip plan, including time of return, with someone reliable. Recognize that accidents can become critical in the wilderness, so travel in a small group provides some security. Stay on trails unless absolutely sure where you are going. Do not expect trails to be well marked. Because the terrain often looks quite different when facing the other way, glance back regularly; that will help you recognize features as you return.

Good clothing, particularly strong footwear, is fundamental; waterproof matches, fire starter, maps, compass, a basic first aid kit, mosquito repellent and rainwear are essentials. Extra food, even on day hikes, may come in handy. Water from lakes, streams and rivers may be of dubious quality. Always boil, treat or filter your drinking water.

Thieves. Do not leave valuables in your car. Vehicles parked at a trailhead are a target for thieves, who operate even during daytime.

Be aware of the danger of being mistaken for a wild animal during hunting season. Hunting is not permitted within any of Vancouver Island's provincial parks.

When traversing glaciers always carry and use adequate lengths of rope and know how to use a rope to effect a crevasse rescue. Watch for hidden crevasses, particularly in the spring or after a snowfall when a thin snow cover may camouflage these hazards.

When hiking in coastal areas, be aware of the possible danger of tsunamis (wave-action from earthquakes) that can sweep inland many kilometres without warning. Surge tides or rogue waves can also occur when an onshore wind combines with a high tide. Be aware of streams whose levels are controlled by dams, where a deluge of water can be released automatically and without warning downstream.

Creatures Great and Small

Those who venture beyond the urban landscape trespass into the back yards of a myriad of native wildlife, animals ranging in size from tiny to intimidating. Mosquitoes and flies can be a serious nuisance. Headnets and an insect repellent will help. Wasps are dangerous. They nest in the ground and in bag-like nests in trees. Many people are allergic to the stings of insects and plants, so pack any necessary antidotes.

There are no wild poisonous snakes on Vancouver Island.

Ticks may be encountered at almost any time of the year, but they are most numerous when the weather warms in late spring. Humans are on the menu of the adult female, who will latch on and drink blood until she is fully engorged. Local ticks are not known to carry Rocky Mountain spotted fever or tick paralysis, but western black-legged ticks, found on Vancouver Island, may carry the bacteria responsible for Lyme disease. A common early symptom of infection is a circular "bull's-eye" rash at the site of the bite. The disease can be cured by antibiotics, but if left untreated it can affect the joints, heart and nervous system. To prevent tick bites, hikers can cover up with long-sleeved shirts and full-length pants secured at the ankle; they can apply insect repellent and they can avoid brushy areas, keeping to open trails.

Recently, *Cryptococcus gattii*, an airborne fungus, has been identified on Vancouver Island. While cases have been rare, the spores can attack the respiratory system (and possibly the nervous system) with pneumonia-like symptoms. Persons whose health is at risk and dogs have been most susceptible. No precautions have been recommended by health authorities.

This is black bear country. Although our resident black bears are rarely encountered (we have 13,000 black bears on the Island, but few grizzly bears), always use discretion in the woods of Vancouver Island, particularly in areas where food, such as berries, is available. Remember, they are not the intruders; we are, and bears defend their personal space, their food and their cubs. Even so, bears will generally do their best to avoid you if they hear you coming, so talking loudly and making other noises when hiking in suspicious areas is advised. Bears have an excellent sense of smell and hearing, and, contrary to popular belief, very good eyesight. It is likely the bear sees you but you remain unaware of its presence. If you do see or hear bears, give them a wide berth and leave the area immediately. If you are actually approached, act large and make lots of noise. Move slowly away and avoid eye contact. A bear can run as fast as a horse, uphill or down, and black bears are good tree-climbers.

When camping, store food away from camp, never in your tent. Hang your food on high, long tree branches. Do not sleep in the clothes you wore to cook food. It is best not to take children or dogs into bear country. The Fish and Wildlife Branch of the BC Ministry of Environment produces a pamphlet: Safety Guide to Bears in the Wild, available on line at: http://www.env.gov.bc.ca/bcparks/explore/misc/bears/bearsaf.html

This is also cougar country, though you can live your whole life here and never see one. A cougar sighting is a rare and treasured event, one to be reported to friends and family. On the other hand, a cougar confrontation is a serious event, one to be reported to a Conservation Officer. Confrontations are extremely rare. Even so, in the last century there have been more than two dozen attacks on humans by cougars on Vancouver Island, with three fatalities. Cougars are big animals, with males weighing 60-90 kg and females, 40-50 kg. They are fast and strong and they are predators. Their prey is primarily deer, but includes other animals, large and small.

Children are probably the most common human target, because their size, sounds and movements resemble those of other prey animals. Cougars are most active at dawn and dusk, but will roam and hunt during any time of the day or night. They may be encountered at any time of the year, but the likelihood of contact increases in late spring and summer when yearlings leave their mother to establish their own territory.

Hike in groups and make your presence known. Keep children in the centre of your group, never running ahead or trailing behind. If you come across cougar prints, scat, or a buried food cache, leave the area immediately. If you actually encounter a cougar, do not run. Stay put and stay calm. Allow the cougar an escape route. Gather up and protect children. Face the animal, maintain eye contact, and make yourself look and sound large, more like a threat than a meal. Stand tall, wave branches; do not crouch or turn your back. If the cougar acts aggressive, stand your ground; if attacked, fight back with any means at your disposal. The Ministry of Environment produces a pamphlet, Safety Guide to Cougars, available on line at: http://www.env.gov.bc.ca/wld/documents/cougsf.htm The cougar and bear pamphlets are also available in the foyer at the Ministry of the Environment regional office at 2080 Labieux Road in Nanaimo.

Vancouver Island supports a small population of gray, or timber, wolves. Although they have a highly developed social order within their packs, they tend to keep to themselves, posing no serious risk to humans.

Unless you are foolish enough to leave food about where they can get at it, you are likely only to be aware of their presence by seeing their footprints, or hearing their eerie howls at night.

The Vancouver Island White-tailed Ptarmigan is a small grouse with distinctive white tail and wings. In winter, all plumage is white. The endemic subspecies on Vancouver Island is on the BC

Vancouver Island White-tailed Ptarmigan. RICK GUTHRIE

provincial Blue List, vulnerable to human and natural disturbance, given its small, isolated populations in the alpine.

A UBC Forestry research project is trying to produce an accurate map of sightings, to determine human interactions. If you sight this bird, fill in a form, often posted at trailheads by the Strathcona Wilderness Institute, or send an informal report to Kathy Martin, 3041-2424 Main Mall, Vancouver, BC, V6T 1Z4, or send an Email to: kmartin@interchange.ubc.ca

Strathcona Park

Strathcona Park was named after Donald Alexander Smith, instrumental in the building of the CPR; knighted in 1866; Member of Parliament, 1871; Governor of the Hudson's Bay Company, 1889; appointed Canada's high commissioner in England, 1896; and made Lord Strathcona and Mount Royal, 1897. Strathcona Park is the oldest of BC's provincial parks, and it contains Vancouver Island's highest peak, the Golden Hinde, and Canada's highest waterfall, Della Falls.

There are trails suitable to hikers of all levels of ability and experience. The descriptions given here and the maps associated with them give information that will allow you to make choices suitable to your ability or that of your group. In Strathcona Park and other areas listed in this guidebook there are destinations that can be reached only by routes, not by trails.

There are many high alpine ridges that interconnect, enabling long traverses and circular tours, for example, from Mount Washington to Rees Ridge and out to Buttle Lake via Flower Ridge, or up from Buttle Lake to Marble Meadows, circling south and returning via Phillips Ridge to Buttle Lake. Those travelling these wilderness routes should be experienced hikers or climbers competent at map reading and route finding, and equipped with map, compass and altimeter. Many hikers also carry a GPS. It is important that you read the preceding Sections, *How To Use This Book*, page 11; and *Hints and Cautions*, page 12, before reading further.

Those who travel in high areas should keep close watch on the weather. Even in summer, a major storm with winds and cold rain, even snow, is possible. Descent to low valleys is wise in the face of deteriorating weather. Use game trails where possible. Flat-bottomed valleys are better for travel than V-shaped valleys.

When climbing a mountain, all ridges converge towards the summit. But descending, especially in cloudy weather, it is easy to miss the right ridge, and end up in the wrong valley. Look backwards often as you climb, and take elevations with an altimeter or mark a waypoint on your GPS at significant junctions.

In the Core Area of Forbidden Plateau (see map M2) camping is permitted only at Kwai Lake, Circlet Lake and Lake Helen Mackenzie, and these sites have pit toilets. Metal food caches are in place at all Forbidden Plateau[1] campsites and the hanging caches have been removed. Campfires are prohibited anywhere in the backcountry of Strathcona Provincial Park. Fires are permitted at designated fire rings at high-use campgrounds (such as the Buttle Lake and Ralph River campsites on Buttle Lake) and various marine sites.

No camping is allowed within one kilometre of any road. BC Parks discourages the marking of routes. The use of paint or permanent markers is illegal. Off-road horse riding and bicycling are not allowed in Strathcona Park and a penalty fine is in place for violations.

There are Fee Collection Zones in Forbidden Plateau Core Area (Map M2), the Elk River Valley (maps M14 and M15), and in the Bedwell Lake, Cream Lake, and Price Creek areas at the south end of Buttle Lake (maps M8 and M11). Fees for camping in the Core Area or in the Fee Collection Zones are $5 per person over age 15, per night (2008).

The BC Parks' pamphlet on Strathcona Provincial Park provides much useful information. Obtain a copy at local tourist infocentres and some sporting goods stores. Maps of the Comox Valley, published by Comox Valley Ground Search and Rescue Association, cover the Forbidden Plateau and Comox Lake areas. (See Map Sources, page 212.)

---

1. **Forbidden Plateau:** From a diary entry by Dr. Robert Brown, who could not persuade local natives to accompany him up the Puntledge River in 1864. See the searchable database at http://ilmbwww.gov.bc.ca/bcnames/

1

Forbidden Plateau
(Wood Mountain)

DESCRIPTION Two public roads lead to Forbidden Plateau, namely, the road to Wood[2] Mountain Provincial Ski Park (site of the burned-down Plateau Ski Lodge), and the now-paved Mount Washington (Strathcona Parkway) road to the Mount Washington Ski Resort and Paradise Meadows. Both routes are accessed from Island Highway 19.

Near Highway 19, Forbidden Plateau Road passes Nymph Falls Regional District Park (55.5 ha), on the Puntledge River. Here you will discover trails for both hikers and mountain bikers. The Outdoor Recreation Council of BC now includes the Puntledge River[3] (part of the Georgia Basin Steelhead Streams) in third place on a list of BC's endangered steelhead rivers.

Logging roads are administered by TimberWest in this area, except that Island Timberland's road to Norm Lake is used to access Gem Lake Trail. Call ahead for current access as various reasons may restrict entry.

The Divers[4]/Rossiter[5] lakes area (1027 ha), near the headwaters of the Oyster River, was added to Forbidden Plateau in 2004, to protect old-growth yellow cedar.

The Forbidden Plateau trails are long-established and offer opportunities for day or overnight hiking. The Comox District Mountaineering

---

2. **Wood Mountain**: Named for the Wood family, builders of the Plateau Lodge, 1933–82. Stuart Wood Island in Moat Lake is named for the eldest son, killed in WW II.

3. **Puntledge River**: Dr. Brown named the river after a now-extinct Salish clan who lived along its banks. Meaning "buried belly", the name has also been rendered as "Pentlatch" and "Puntluch".

4. **Divers Lake:** The name comes from the loons ("hell-divers") who inhabit the lake.

5. **Rossiter Lake:** Len Rossiter was an early guide to Forbidden Plateau.

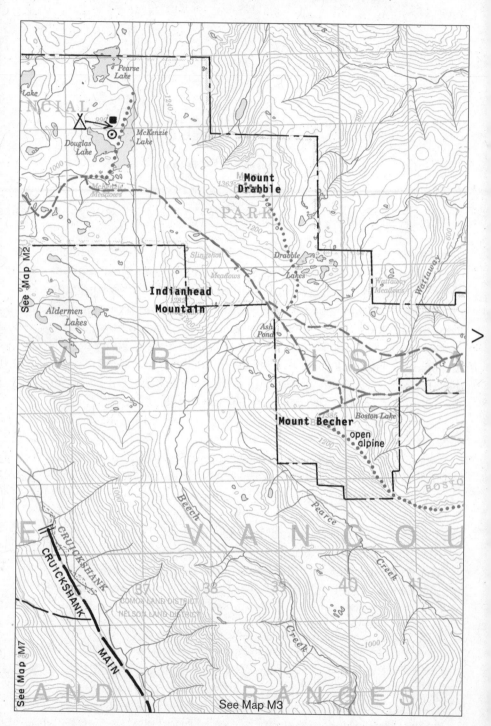

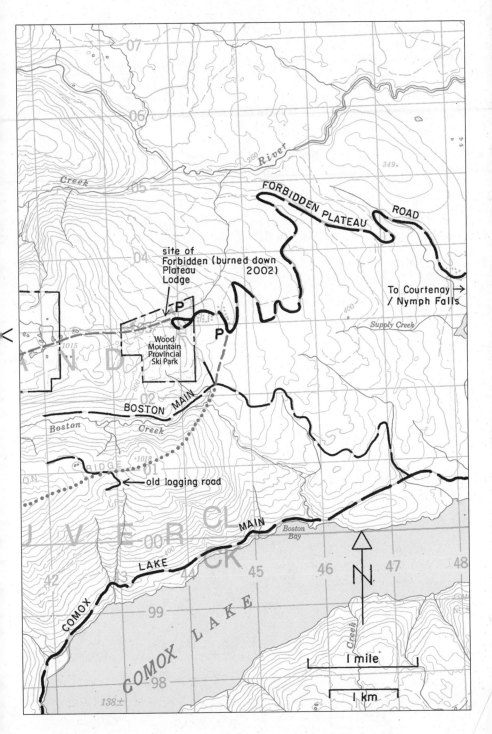

Club (CDMC) and BC Parks have erected signs on trees at trail junctions. Remember that trails can become hard to follow in this unique alpine area and it is easy to take a wrong fork.

ACCESS   For the Wood Mountain access to Forbidden Plateau, from Highway 19 take Exit 127 to Piercy Road and turn right. From Courtenay, it is about 19 km to the Plateau Ski Lodge parking area.

1.a Mount Becher   Map M1

DESCRIPTION The Mount Becher[6] Trail is a great choice for a day hike. A good, well-defined trail leads from the site of the burnt-out Plateau Ski Lodge (razed by vandals in 2002) to Mount Becher. At the ski hill and later, nearer Mount Becher there is substantial elevation gain.

TRAIL   It is about 9 km from the trailhead west to Mount Becher and back. More experienced hikers can head back from Mount Becher (1385 m) following a rugged, sometimes hard-to-locate route via the Boston Ridge. (Looping back this way adds 4 km and some difficulty to your hike.) The route is fairly steep in places, particularly where it drops from the ridge to Boston Creek[7] and the Boston Main logging road. Continue along an old rail grade back up to the Plateau road, at a switchback, just below the lodge site. This route was originally constructed and flagged by CDMC.

---

6. **Mount Becher,** and Becher Bay, near Victoria, are named for Captain Alexander Bridport Becher (1796-1876), a respected surveying officer of the Royal Navy.
7. **Boston Creek**, Lake, Ridge: E.J. "Boston" Calman (who once lived in Boston) of Happy Valley near Cumberland, had a cabin at Boston Bay, Comox Lake.

2

Forbidden Plateau
(Paradise Meadows)

Take the Mount Washington Road (also called the Strathcona Parkway) from Highway 19 and follow the signs to the ski resort. Turn left onto the road to the Nordic Lodge and continue another 2.5 km to the parking area near the Raven Lodge. From Courtenay to the start of the trails is about 25 km.

Mount Washington was named after Rear Admiral John Washington (RN) Secretary of the Royal Geographical Society, and who succeeded Sir Francis Beaufort as Hydrographer in 1855.

2.a Paradise Meadows[8] Loop   Map M2

TRAIL This trail starts at Mount Washington's Raven Lodge parking lot and runs down to the brown bridge on the old Battleship Lake Trail, then returns on the other side of Paradise Creek—length 2.2 km. This trail, roughly the smallest wintertime cross-country ski loop, is a beautiful walk suitable for all ages. The trail is mostly boardwalk.

2.b Helen Mackenzie Loop   Map M2

DESCRIPTION This trail from Paradise Meadows winds gently through rolling meadows to bring walkers of almost any level of ability to Lake Helen Mackenzie[9]. This pleasant loop requires about three hours, not including rest stops.

---

8. **Paradise Meadows:** Named by C.S. Wood when he was exploring the Dove Creek Trail in 1928.
9. **Lake Helen McKenzie:** Helen assisted her uncle, Lt. Gov. Randolf Bruce, when he opened the Dove Creek Trail in 1929.

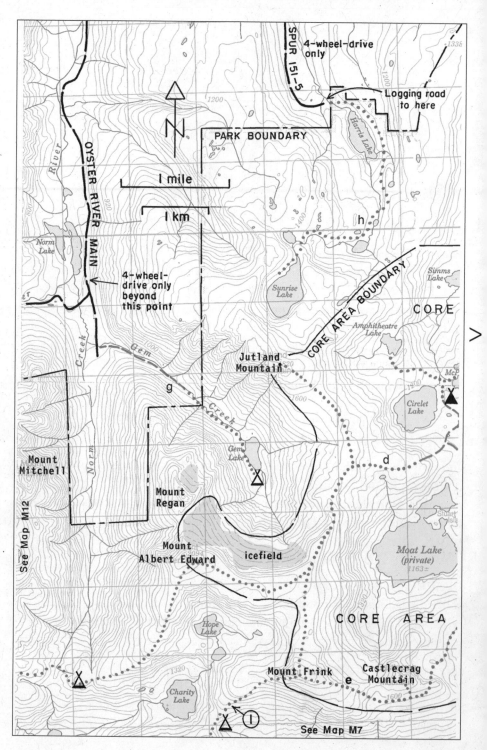

Map M2 Forbidden Plateau (Paradise Meadows)

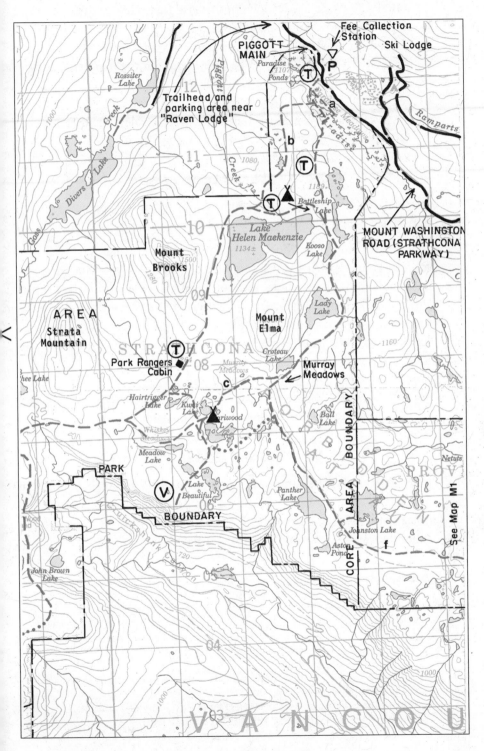

TRAIL From Paradise Meadows trailhead at Raven Lodge hike south and west, climbing slowly up Piggott Creek 2.9 km to the shore of Lake Helen Mackenzie. Following the lakeshore trail eastwards (ie. to the left) leads to the west side of Battleship Lake where you join the main trail back to Paradise Meadows.

NOTE At Lake Helen Mackenzie there is a well-developed campsite. Core area camping fees apply.

2.c Kwai Lake Loop   Map M2

DESCRIPTION A longer hike, but in gentle terrain sprinkled with lakes and varied meadowland.

TRAIL At Lake Helen Mackenzie (see Section 2.b) turn west (right) to follow a rough but easy grade trail which ascends to subalpine meadows near the Park Rangers' cabin, and your first good views of Mount Albert Edward and Mount Regan. Turn left at Hairtrigger[10] Lake and pass Kwai Lake[11] on your left, a very beautiful and rewarding destination. To return, follow signs to Croteau[12] Lake, and from there to Battleship Lake[13]. This loop requires a full day.

NOTE Kwai is the second campsite in the core area, well developed with tent pads, toilets and food caches. Core area camping fees apply.

2.d Mount Albert Edward[14]   Map M2

DESCRIPTION The summit (2094 m elevation) is about six hours from the parking lot, one way. A developed campsite exists at Circlet Lake and it is a good place to stop before a steep climb onto the ridge leading to Albert Edward—especially if carrying full packs.

---

10. **Hairtrigger Lake:** Clinton Wood named the lake after he missed his shot at a deer.
11. *Kwai* means "wood" in a local native language, and this multi-lingual pun refers to the C.S. Wood family, pioneers of camps and trails on Forbidden Plateau.
12. **Croteau Lake:** Eugene Croteau of Comox established Croteau Camp after the Dove Creek Trail was opened, providing tent sites and a central cabin with cooking and dining facilities.
13. **Battleship Lake** was named by Clinton Wood after his son noted the resemblance of the trees and islands to a battleship.
14. **Mount Albert Edward** was named after Queen Victoria's eldest son, who ascended the throne as Edward VII after her death in 1901.

TRAIL From the Rangers' cabin (Section 2.c above) maintain your elevation to pass Hairtrigger Lake on your left. Another hour brings you to a short side trail leading to Circlet Lake. The trail becomes a route after the shoulder and tarns (small mountain lakes) at 1400 m.

NOTE Many groups camp at Circlet Lake and travel light for a summit day-return (6 km and four hours one way). Remember to pack for a long day, and carry what you will need for exposed ridge travel and sudden weather changes.

2.e Castlecrag Loop   Map M2

DESCRIPTION This is a high alpine loop around a spectacular peak that connects with routes to the south. For most hikers this is a day hike to complete the loop from Circlet Lake. Ambitious hikers can scramble to the summit for a panorama view, but best to avoid the precarious subsidiary peak near the summit.

TRAIL On the Mount Albert Edward trail (Section 2.d above) turn left past Circlet Lake and hike past Moat Lake on your right. On a route that involves some steep sections, circle Castlecrag Mountain on your right. Pass the scrambling route to the summit near the south side of the peak. After the possible summit side trip, continue the climb westward to the gentle summit of Mount Frink, then bear right (north) to rejoin the Mount Albert Edward trail and return to Circlet Lake.

2.f Mount Becher to Paradise Meadows
Map M2 (also map M1)

DESCRIPTION This trail traverses from the Forbidden Plateau area to connect with the access from Mount Washington area, and thus requires transport at both ends.

TRAIL From the base of the north slope of Mount Becher (Map M1), travel across plateau terrain between Indianhead Mountain on your left, passing a route to Mount Drabble on your right. Angling westward at a meadow, pass a stream to McKenzie[15] Lake, where you can make a side trip north along the lake to a cabin, cairn and campsite (no facilities)

---

15. **McKenzie Lake:** Named for John McKenzie, mayor of Courtenay during time that water rights were obtained and a dam was built (1929).

between McKenzie and Douglas[16] lakes. Continuing west and then north, pass between Johnston and Panther lakes, eventually rejoining the Kwai Lake Loop (Map M2) in Murray Meadows. The Mount Washington trailhead is about 6 km from this junction.

2.g Gem Lake   Map M2

ACCESS This trail is accessed from Oyster Bay on Highway 19, via logging roads up the Oyster River to Norm Lake[17]. A staffed security gate at Mile 16 ensures the road is closed to the public until 5 pm weekdays. It is open most weekends. Check with the Island Timberlands office in Campbell River. (Appendix, page 215.)

TRAIL From Norm Lake, a trail/route follows the grown-in road south to Gem Creek[18] coming in from the left, then follows the west side of Gem Creek to Gem Lake, where there is a camping option. This trail was constructed by CDMC.

2.h Sunrise Lake   Map M2

ACCESS Just south of the Oyster River bridge, turn off the Duncan Bay Main onto Oyster River Main. (This is not the same road as the Island Timberlands Oyster River Main on the north side of the river.) Head southwest for roughly 10 km and turn right onto Rossiter Main, travelling for 5 km to a bridge over Piggott Creek[19] (Branch 151-5). After the bridge, pass through a gate, locked on weekdays, but open most weekends. (Contact TimberWest; see Appendix, page 215.) Turn north across a bridge over Harris Creek. Stay on the west side of this creek to road's end (8 km) just west of the outfall of Harris Lake[20].

ROUTE Cross the creek to the start of the route, which follows the east side of Harris Lake and generally the outflow creek from Sunrise Lake.

---

16. **Douglas Lake:** Named for William (Bill) Douglas, a Courtenay alderman who stocked Douglas and McKenzie lakes with trout. He was remembered by children of the 1930s, as he bought cascara bark and beer bottles, their only source of income.
17. **Norm Lake** is named for Norm Stewart, BCLS, who surveyed the Forbidden Plateau area and named many of its features, 1934-35.
18. **Gem Creek, Lake:** Originally named "Emerald Lake" by the Regan (E&N) Survey in 1930.
19. **Piggott Creek,** for Julian A. Piggott, Helen MacKenzie's fiancé.
20. **Harris Lake,** named for a trapper who lived in Courtenay.

3

Comox Creek

3.a Alone Mountain   Map M3

DESCRIPTION This makes a nice spring hike since the snow goes off the southern slope a few weeks earlier than on other mountains. In clear weather there are good views of Comox Glacier. The spring flowers are always beautiful and there are wild onions in season. This trail was built and marked by CDMC.

Before your hike call TimberWest for current information. (Appendix, page 215.) In the Comox Lake and Creek area, TimberWest hauls along area mainlines, so public access is usually restricted to weekends and holidays only, or after 6 pm on weekdays. Check at the watchman's security station, just up the road from the dam at the foot of Comox Lake. There are currently no entry fees charged.

ACCESS From the causeway and dam at the foot of Comox Lake, drive approximately 13.5 km along TimberWest's Comox Lake Main to just before the top of the hill near the Cruickshank River bridge. Watch for a sign saying "Heliport 15 and Alone Mountain Trail." A very short logging road leads in toward Alone Mountain.

TRAIL At the end of the road look for a big hole on the right, where a large boulder has been removed. Blue paint and an arrow indicate the start of the trail. Follow the trail west and then north to the top of Alone Mountain (847 m).

3.b Idiens/Capes Lakes
Map M3 (also map M7, page 46)

DESCRIPTION This trail/route provides a stimulating hike, good swimming in hot weather and wonderful views of Comox Glacier. Allow five hours, one way, for the ascent. There is also a side trail, easily followed, to the summit of Mount Ginger Goodwin[21].

ACCESS From the causeway and dam at the foot of Comox Lake, take Comox Lake Main for 14.5 km to the Cruickshank[22] River bridge. On the south side of the river, swing right, down to the river and follow Cruickshank Main approximately 3 km to where there is a most magnificent view of Comox Glacier.(35) Turn left (south) onto South Main for 0.5 km to a large, cleared log sorting area, on the right. The trail begins in the southwest corner, near an old logging road. There is no longer any vehicle access up this steep spur, so park at the bottom.

TRAIL/ROUTE At first the trail follows part way up the old logging road until it reaches a bench overlooking Comox Creek and the Cruickshank River. Instead of following the old road at this point and going up the east side of the slope, the trail now continues straight ahead and climbs, via several switchbacks, up the south side of Mount Ginger Goodwin through a stand of trees. The trail is well marked, with flagging tape and a series of blue paint marks.

The route leads around the south side of Idiens[23] Lake to Lee Plateau, where camping is possible and there are good views of the rough country to the west. Continue south down to Capes[24] Creek, avoiding the few cliffs. The Capes memorial cairn and plaque are just before the outfall of Capes Creek. From Capes Creek go roughly southeast up to Capes Ridge for excellent views of Comox Glacier. Return via Capes Lake, branching right directly to the Idiens/Capes Lakes junction and then out the way you came in.

NOTE Even though the end of Capes Ridge shows on the map as being near South Main road, it is a precarious trip down to the road, with huge belts of cliffs which are nearly impossible to avoid, and this method of return is definitely not recommended.

---

21. **Ginger Goodwin** was a labour leader in the coal mines, including Cumberland, who opposed World War I and was killed by police, trying to enforce his draft call to the army.
22. **Cruickshank River**, named for George Cruickshank, Honourable Secretary of the committee for the Vancouver Island Exploration Expedition (VIEE) of 1864.
23. **Idiens Lake**, named for Richard Idiens, president of CDMC, killed in WW II. Cairn erected at lake.
24. **Geoff Capes** missed by one day being first to climb the Golden Hinde. (Preceded by the surveyor, N.C. Stewart.)

Map M3 Comox Creek

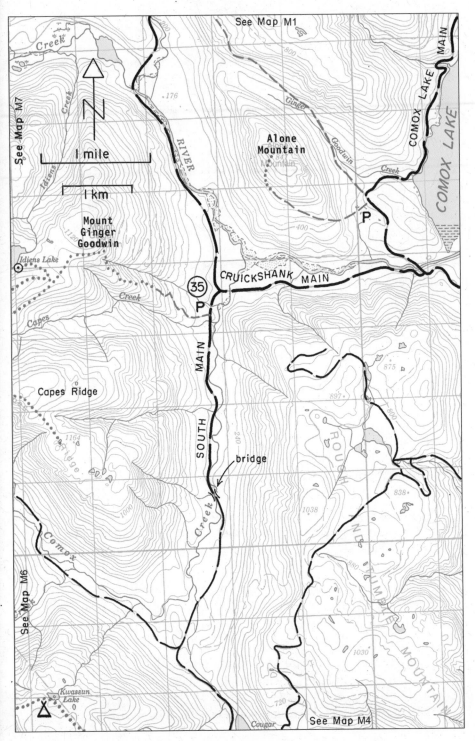

See Map M1

Creek

N
1 mile
1 km

See Map M7

RIVER

176

800

Ginger

Alone
Mountain

Goodwin

Creek

COMOX LAKE MAIN

COMOX LAKE

P

Mount
Ginger
Goodwin

1120

Idiens Lake

400

Creek

35
P

CRUICKSHANK MAIN

Capes

875

Capes Ridge

897

600

1164

SOUTH

MAIN

240

bridge

ROUGH

838

1000

Creek

1038

Comox

See Map M6

980

RUMPLE

MOUNTAIN

1030

Kwassun
Lake

Cougar

See Map M4

4

Forbush and Willemar Lakes

DESCRIPTION This area includes access to some lovely lakes, including canoe routes, generally on TimberWest roads from the Comox Lake area to the north.

The southern access along the Ash River from Elsie Lake leads to Oshinow Lake and provides convenient routes on Island Timberlands roads into the south part of Strathcona Park.

Through access from Port Alberni to Comox Lake via the Valley Link Highway and Toma Main is now closed.

4.a June, Junior and Toy Lakes
Map M4 (also map M5)

ACCESS To reach these lakes via Oshinow[25] Lake, travel northwest about 20 km on Beaver Creek Road from Port Alberni, then on Sommers Road for 2 km and left on a main logging road, drive about 9 km, crossing Lanterman Creek. Check conditions with Island Timberlands, (Appendix, page 215). Within about 1 km turn west onto a branch road, drive 5 km staying left, then turn right at a T-intersection to cross the Ash River. Follow the Ash River Main, passing Turnbull Lake on the left and then Elsie Lake on the right. After crossing the Ash River to its north side, drive 8.5 km, and turn right. Do not cross the Ash again. After about 3 km turn right onto Branch 110, a rocky road, suited to four wheel drive vehicles. (See Section 5.a)

Access to the east end of Branch 110 from the Long Lake Road along the north side of Elsie Lake is often impassable.

---

25. **Oshinow Lake**: From the local word meaning "all kinds of game."

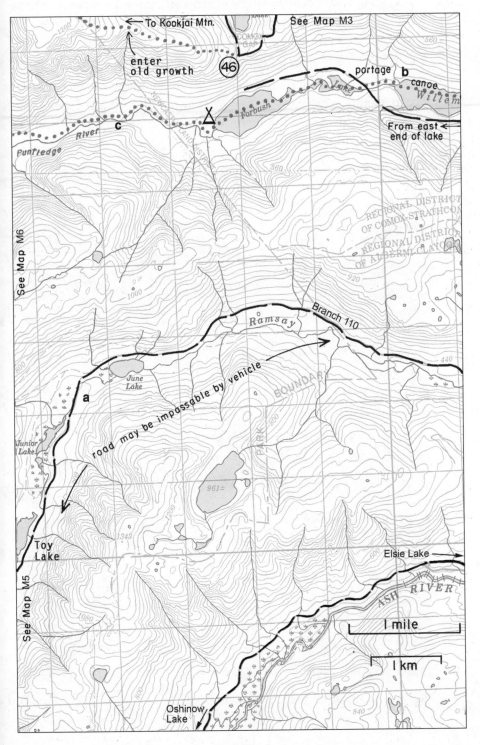

Camping and boat launching is possible on the south shore of Oshinow Lake, just north of the creek that drains into Oshinow Lake from Toy Lake.

TRAIL From Oshinow Lake, hike a few kilometres northeast along a logging road to three small lakes, in succession, Toy, Junior, and June lakes. A short spur road goes to Toy Lake. At Junior Lake a small trail along the old road leads 200 m to the lakeshore. June Lake is adjacent to the road.

Rugged mountains border Willemar Lake.   RICHARD BLIER

4.b Forbush[26] and Willemar[27] Lakes
Map M4 (also map M6)

DESCRIPTION Also known in the past as "The Little Lakes," these lakes are suitable for canoe travel, with a short portage or "lining" section between the lakes. The best camping place is at the top of Forbush Lake (west end) on the remains of an old cat-logging road that stopped at the Park boundary.

ACCESS A new logging road extends around Willemar Lake and along the Forbush Lakes. There is restricted public access on TimberWest logging roads along Comox Lake. Drive on these logging roads past the south end of Comox Lake, driving south up the Puntledge River when the Toma Main turns left (east), then continue to the foot of Willemar Lake.

CANOE ROUTE Paddle to the top end of Willemar Lake and drag your canoe up the channel (about 200m) or take the portage trail on the left. ("It's right where you need it," says Ruth Masters, who helped put it in). Relaunch for a short paddle through an "everglades" marshy area leading into Forbush Lake.

4.c Puntledge River   Map M4 (also map M6)

TRAIL At the camping area at the west end of Forbush Lake, hike on the old road, which has now softened into a pleasant trail, west into the magnificent old growth forest of the Upper Puntledge. After about 2 km there is a delightful rest spot at a waterfall. From there on, the trail has been allowed to grow over, though it is a reasonable route through open timber all the way to Puntledge Lake.

NOTES From here there are feasible and challenging route possibilities to the Ash River and over to Drinkwater Creek[28]. One can also connect with the route to Red Pillar. (Section 5.a)

---

26. **Forbush Lake:** Edward Howe Forbush was an ornithologist in the Comox District.
27. **Willemar Lake:** Reverend J. X. Willemar, first Roman Catholic priest in the Comox District.
28. **Drinkwater Creek** was named for Joe Drinkwater, a trapper and area miner.

5

Oshinow Lake

5.a Oshinow Lake and Red Pillar
Map M5 (also map M6)

DESCRIPTION This route provides more direct access to the Red Pillar and the Cliffe Glacier than the traditional route to the Comox Glacier from the east, (Sections 6.b and 6.c) or via Flower or Henshaw ridges from the west, (Section 6.d). In addition, it is a rewarding hike in its own right, though steep and on an undeveloped route, about 5 hours from vehicle to camp, with pleasant high ridge camping near Esther Lake.

ACCESS Section 4.a, page 32, for access to Oshinow Lake. After 2 km, turn left onto branch 110H, at a sign "RDPIL." From here it is 5 km to a slide blocking the road. The trail begins on the north side of the blockage.

TRAIL/ROUTE Where the road ends in a slide, over half way along the north side of the lake, hike northwest above Oshinow Lake, and then beside the Ash River[29]. A steep route climbs north to the ridge west of Puntledge Lake. Stay on the southwest side and above Esther Lake. (This area of the park is zoned Wilderness Conservation which means that no established trails are allowed.)

The route is in the alpine zone and is not technical following the upper bench on the ridge above Esther Lake, map M6. Nearing the Red Pillar[30], traverse from the south side to the west side and gain a bench at 1900 m elevation to access the Cliffe Glacier. ⑨

---

29. **Ash River:** Dr. John Ash of the committee for Vancouver Island Exploration Expedition of 1864.
30. **The Red Pillar:** Ben Hughes of the Argus newspaper wrote that Geoff Capes and Jack Gregson climbed the mountain in 1931 and left a note in the summit cairn suggesting the name "The Pillar."

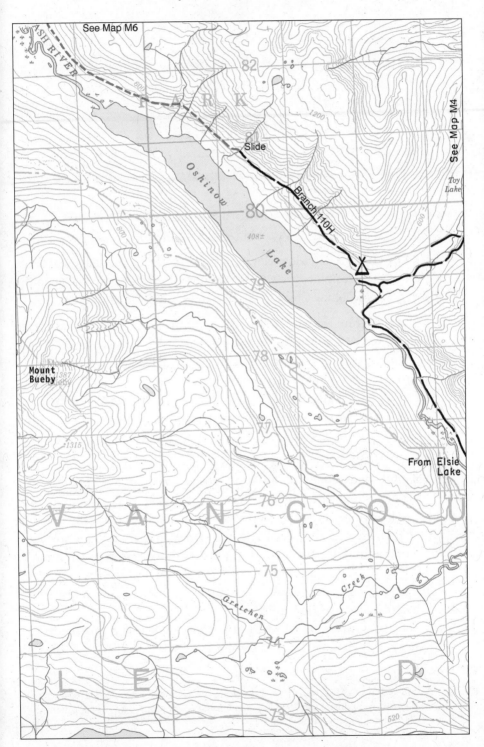

See Map M6

ASH RIVER

P A R K

Slide

Branch 110H

Oshinow Lake

82

1200

80

408±

79

78

77

76

75

73

600

600

800

520

See Map M4

Toy Lake

From Elsie Lake

Mount Bueby

1387

1315

V A N C O U

L E D

Gretchen Creek

6

Comox Glacier

6.a Century Sam Lake[31]
Map M6 (Also Map M3)

DESCRIPTION This low-elevation trail to Century Sam Lake starts just west of the stream crossing ㊱ for Comox Glacier Trail and goes up the south side of Comox Creek to the lake and a nice little campsite.

ACCESS From the causeway and dam at the foot of Comox Lake, take TimberWest's Comox Lake Main, then right on Cruickshank Main, about 17.5 km to the junction with South Main.㉟ Cut left and take South Main approximately 7 km to a junction where the road to Cougar Lake swings off to the left (southeast). Keep right (northwest) to the end of the road. About 200 m from the end of the road, park on the side of the road and make sure you leave room for others to turn around.

TRAIL Hike down to the stream and cross to the Comox Glacier Trail.㊱ The trail winds along Comox Creek's south side to the bottom of the first avalanche slide path. Thick spring vegetation can make the route here hard to see. The trail angles up slightly and enters the forest again and then into a second slide area. The trail angles up again into the trees and out into a third avalanche slide area. Next comes a steep ascent into the forest and a section of windfall. The trail eventually emerges at the river just below Century Sam Lake where there are some rough campsites and a memorial cairn to Sid Williams.

The trail, made by CDMC in the 1960s, is brushed out seasonally. Expect windfall in the upper section below the lake after winter. The trail

---

31. **Sid Williams** of Courtenay was a climber, prospector and actor. He played **Century Sam** during the 1958 B.C. Centennial celebrations. The Lake was named in 1961 and a cairn has been built.

can be difficult to find at the bottom of the avalanche paths when the bushes are thick over the summer.

6.b Comox Glacier   Map M6

DESCRIPTION This trail is a steep ascent to the 1240 m level, a ridge walk on a route across to Black Cat Mountain with fine views of Comox[32] Glacier and of Century Sam Lake below. Past the north shoulder of Black Cat Mountain, there is a descent to Lone Tree Pass and a direct scramble up to the south end of Comox Glacier. The trail was built by CDMC in the early 1960s.

This trip is only for strong hikers and should be made in reasonable weather. It is a good three-day hike: one day to the "frog pond" campsite (about 1.5 km along the ridge), a second day travelling light up to the glacier and back to camp, and a third day to pack out.

ACCESS As for the preceding section, Century Sam Lake, take Timber-West's Comox Lake Main, then Cruickshank Main, then South Main south about 7 km and turn right (northwest) where the Cougar Lake turn goes left, continuing to the parking area within about 200 m from the end of the road. You can seasonally make the journey in a two wheel drive vehicle, but might need a high clearance vehicle for the last 2 km of the road.

TRAIL From the end of the road (36) hike down to Comox Creek, and take the log crossing to a section of trail with switchbacks. Unfortunately this only goes about a quarter of the way up and there is a lot of work to do to gain the ridge. About a kilometre along the ridge, just before the "frog ponds", there is a col or saddle that hikers must negotiate. Descend from the ridge on the south side. The route is steep and exposed and there is loose rock.

After the "frog ponds", the trail becomes a rough route up to the glacier. Cross a wide flat snowfield to a cairn. In places the rock steps can be quite intimidating, especially to inexperienced hikers. There are several spots where some hikers might prefer to be roped.

> **NOTE** If you are travelling on the Comox Glacier, read the caution concerning glacier travel given on page 42.

---

32. **Comox** is a shortened word for "abundance" (of game or berries) in the Yaculta (Euclataw) dialect.

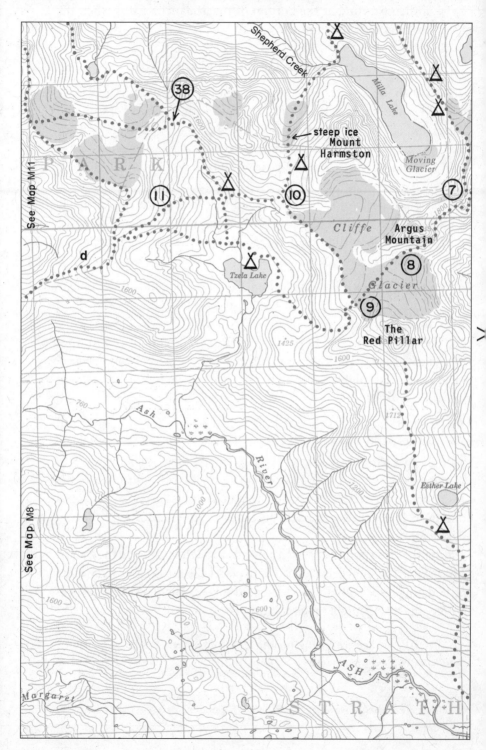

Map M6 Comox Glacier

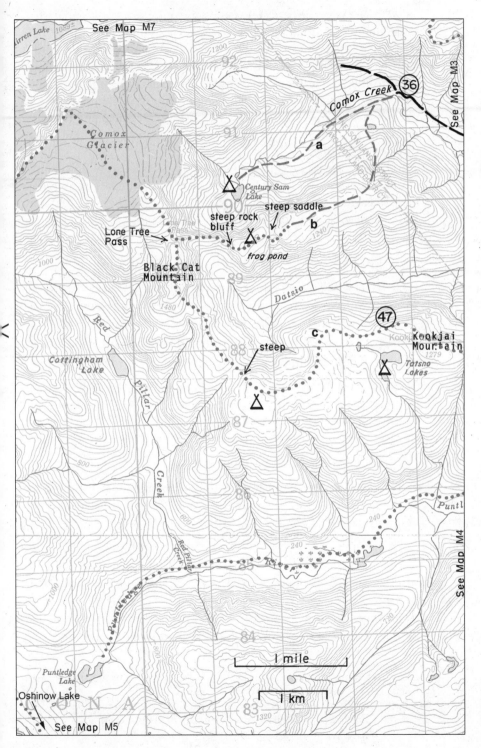

See Map M7
See Map M3
See Map M4
See Map M5

Irren Lake 1089±

92

Comox Creek

36

Comox Glacier

91

a

90

Century Sam Lake

steep saddle

b

Lone Tree Pass

steep rock bluff

frog pond

Black Cat Mountain

1480

89

Datsio

47

c

Kookjai

Kookjai Mountain

1279

88

steep

Red Pillar

Cottingham Lake

Tatsno Lakes

87

1000

Pillar

Creek

800

86

600

Puntl

240

Red Pillar Creek

240

1720

Peters Watershed

84

1000

800

1 mile

1 km

Puntledge Lake

83 1320

Oshinow Lake

T O N A

1200

1240

41

NOTE Ice axes, ropes and crevasse rescue equipment are essential when traversing icefields and active glaciers such as the Comox and Cliffe glaciers. While crevasses for the most part are obvious, in the spring or after a snowfall, they may be thinly covered and hazardous to both the uninitiated and the experienced. There have been small accidents on Comox Glacier, but no crevasse fatalities, as yet. Be prepared and ultra-cautious. Since fog can close in quickly, carry map and compass, especially on the featureless glacier, and escape to the trailhead in any threatening weather.

Backpacking gear is required, including a portable stove for cooking, as fires are prohibited in the Park backcountry. No-impact camping is a preferable goal. There is a lack of available water on the ridge until you reach small streams off the glacier.

6.c Kookjai[33] Mountain   Map M6 (also map M4)

DESCRIPTION Though a longer access to Comox Glacier, the Kookjai Mountain route crosses a lovely plateau area and avoids having to negotiate the exposed rock sections of the "frog pond" route. There is pleasant camping at Tatsno Lakes, ㊼ a very beautiful location with good tent sites and view, or at Kwassun Lake ("star" in local dialect) where there is good access to clean water and perhaps less "buggy" than the Tatsno Lakes.

ACCESS Drive in from the foot of Comox Lake as described for Century Sam Lake (Section 6.a) but keep left (southeast) at the Cougar Lake turn on South Main. At Comox Gap ㊻ the road turns sharply to the east on its way to Rough and Tumble Mountain. This is where the trail begins.

TRAIL It is an easy walk up an old logging road for about 1 km and then a well-marked trail from there. Follow the backbone of the ridge right up above the tree line. From here it is possible to hike to Comox Glacier following a system of ridges leading to Black Cat Mountain[34], after which you join the Comox Glacier Route from the "frog ponds" (Section 6.b) at Lone Tree Pass. This makes for a very long trek, so if you can go further on your first day you will shorten your second.

The route from Kookjai Mountain (1279 m) to the base of Black Cat Mountain is easy and well defined with numerous tarns and places

---

33. **Kookjai Mountain**: Norm Stewart applied the local word for "to see", this being the first place to view Comox Glacier on this route.
34. **Black Cat Mountain**: A 1920s hiking group attributed their improved weather on this climb to a black cat that crossed their path near Courtenay.

to camp. A good (low-impact) camp can be made at 1400 m, up on the ridge summit, west of Tatsno Lakes. Shortly after beginning the climb up Black Cat Mountain there are bluffs that turn to the right and then it is necessary to zigzag through further bluffs to the alpine. Take note of your route through the bluffs as it can be tricky finding your way back down Black Cat Mountain towards Kookjai Mountain.

6.d Cliffe Glacier to Flower Ridge
Map M6 (also map M8)

DESCRIPTION This is a remote mountain route that provides access to (or exit from) the glaciated region of the Comox and Cliffe[35] glaciers. It can be linked to Henshaw—Shepherd ridge from Buttle Lake in the west or to routes along Rees Ridge from the Mount Washington region in the north. There are views from the route to the higher peaks of Strathcona Park in the west and to the glacier region to the east. The ridge can be exposed to severe weather, even in summer.

This description is given from Cliffe Glacier, west to the south end of Flower Ridge (Section 11.d). The route can be reversed, but it is not so direct a route to the glaciers region as from the Ash River, Oshinow Lake (Section 5.a) or from the "frog ponds" route, (Section 6.b).

ROUTE From the west side of The Red Pillar,⑨ there are two routes to Tzela Lake (meaning heart, for the shape of the lake). The first starts down near the base of the steep part of The Red Pillar, and into a small side valley leading down to the meadows on the east side of the lake. This is the best route for going to the lake only. The second route goes down a small ridge alongside the glacier. Keep to the glacier side near the lower end and cross the creek below the snout. If the creek is very high you will have to wade it. Go into the timber facing the end of the ridge, find a game trail about 15 m above the creek and, staying high, well above the creek, ⑩ contour around till you reach an open area. Follow this around to the open flower slopes that angle down to the northwest, and to the large upper flower meadows on the main valley floor. From these meadows, southwards down to Tzela Lake, there is a good game trail which stays on the east side of the stream and leads to camping areas at the north end of the lake. If heading for Flower Ridge, stay high and connect to the ridge west of Tzela Lake.

---

35. **Cliffe Glacier:** Lucius Cliffe was the first white boy born north of Nanaimo.

The Flower Ridge route goes west, across the meadows at about the 1280 m level and, staying to the left of a small side creek and contouring around on open slopes,⑪ goes up the ridge to the 1540 m level. This upper route will avoid the bushy sections encountered on the lower route starting at Tzela Lake. From here, follow the watershed ridge between the Ash River and Henshaw Creek, southwest to intersect Flower Ridge from the north. Proceed southwest until you can see down into the Price Creek Valley, then turn northwest onto the narrow connector to Flower Ridge, (Section 11.d).

Milla Lake looking north to Rees Ridge.   GIL PARKER

7

Rees Ridge

The route from the Mount Washington area of Forbidden Plateau to the glacier region of the southern part of Strathcona Park has long been a favourite for serious backcountry hikers and climbers. Leading from the Mount Albert Edward trail south along a watershed that divides runoff from the Cruickshank River on the east and the rivers draining into Buttle Lake on the west, the ridge route traverses the Aureole Icefield[36] and Rees Ridge, arriving at the Comox and Cliffe glacier region, with options to exit from the mountains east, west or south.

Recently, there has been further exploration and development of routes to this salient ridge from the east, via the Carey Lakes region. (See Section 7.b) All of these options require route finding skills and thorough knowledge of backcountry navigation. Depending upon the route chosen toward the south of this route, climbing techniques may be needed.

7.a Mount Albert Edward to Rees[37] Ridge
Map M7 (also maps M2 page 24, for north approach, and M6, page 40, for south.)

DESCRIPTION This is another tough, high alpine route along barren ridges. There is a rugged beauty to the terrain, interesting geology on the ridges and repeated scenic panoramas. (This description will take you to Tzela Lake, connecting to Section 6.d)

ROUTE The route leaves the main route to Mount Albert Edward (Section 2.d) at the 1880 m level, where it turns west towards that summit.

---

36. Originally named Aureole Snowfield in 1935 for its halo effect, renamed **Aureole Icefield** in 1980.
37. **Rees** was a prospector who died at the age of 75 on the Mount Becher Trail in winter 1933.

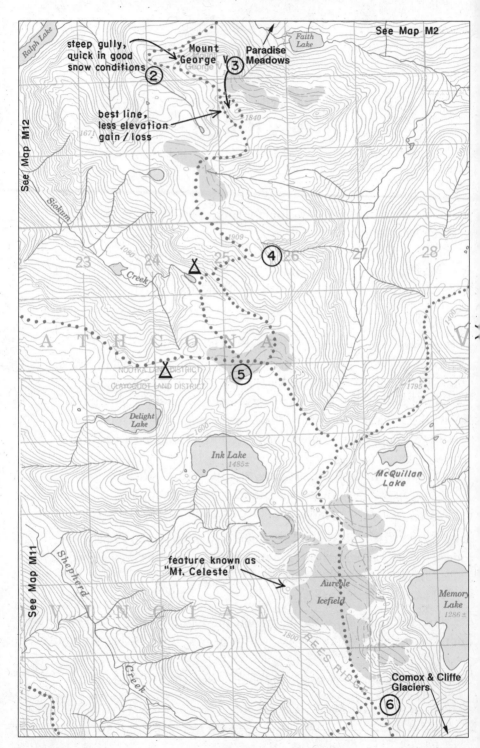

See Map M2

steep gully,
quick in good
snow conditions

Mount
George V

Paradise
Meadows

Faith
Lake

Ralph Lake

② ③

best line,
less elevation
gain / loss

1840

See Map M12

Siokum

1090

1067

1909

④

23 24 Creek 25 26 27 28

A T H C O N A

NOOTKA LAND DISTRICT
CLAYOQUOT LAND DISTRICT

⑤

1795

Delight
Lake

1600

Ink Lake
1485±

McQuillan
Lake

See Map M11

Shepherd

V I N C I A L

feature known as
"Mt. Celeste"

Aureole
Icefield

Memory
Lake
1286±

1800 R E E S R I D G E

Creek

Comox & Cliffe
Glaciers

⑥

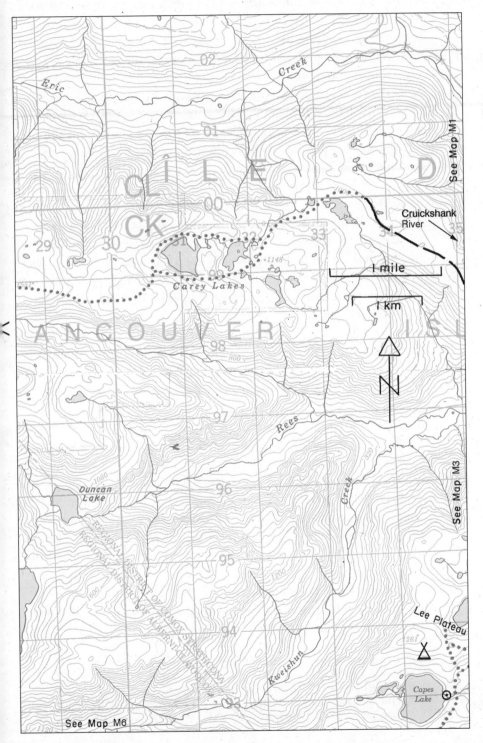

See Map M1

Cruickshank River

1 mile

1 km

N

Eric

Creek

CL Î L E   D

CK

Carey Lakes

ANCOUVER   ISL

Rees

Creek

Duncan Lake

Kweishun

Lee Plateau

Capes Lake

See Map M3

See Map M6

Follow the height of land south, up the north side of Mount Frink (the 1960 m ridge west of Castlecrag), go left around the summit rocks and down the centre of the west ridge. Stick to the southeast side of the buttress where there are fewer bluffs and contour into the col. Do not turn south too soon or you will run into cliffs. At about the 1600 m level ① above the steep section east of Charity Lake, turn south and follow ledges back to regain the centre of the ridge at about the 1540 m level. Continue down the ridge to a good campsite just below the col between Faith Lake and Charity Lake[38]. Allow about five hours hiking time from the trailhead at Mount Washington.

Follow around the north peak of Mount George V, on open areas up to the 1630 m level, then contour west across the mountain's north slope or snowfield. At the steep drop-off on the west ridge ② turn sharp left and follow up this well-defined ridge to about 1810 m, then contour below the steep section and head south towards the main summit. You can avoid the summit by turning west and descending a rockslide, then back up to the ridge, or you can go up and over the summit, ③ (and more elevation gain and loss) which is not as hard as it looks.

Proceeding south from Mount George V[39], follow the height of land. As you near the col at the head of Siokum Creek, (meaning "in the sun") a cliff band ahead (not shown on the map) blocks the direct route to the col. A game trail contours to the right from about 1870 m down to 1810 m right ④ [10U325345/5499623NAD83] [10U325339/5499398NAD27] where you descend sharply to the west in a small slide area. Drop about 400 m to a small lake at the head of the creek, a good place to camp.

To rejoin the ridge, hike south up easy contours west of a bluff to a point between two bumps. This is easier than going back up to the col, which will be on your left. At this point, marked ⑤ on the map M7, you connect with a route from Ralph River that can be used as a viable escape route. The main route south continues on a height of land between Ink Lake[40] and McQuillan[41] Lake and on to Aureole snowfield. Follow a line of rock cairns, positioned where necessary to avoid steep sections. Hike south up the snowfield to a low point between the summits of Rees Ridge, then head roughly southeast down the main ridge towards the col between Milla Lake (meaning "white" in native language) and Mirren[42] Lake.

---

38. Of the three lakes, **Faith, Hope and Charity**, Charity Lake is the greatest.
39. **Mount George V**, named for the King in 1935 on his silver jubilee.
40. **Ink Lake,** named by Sid Williams, for its dark colour.
41. **McQuillan Lake:** RCAF Flight Lieutenant Murray McQuillan was killed in W.W. II.
42. **Mirren Lake**, named after Mirren Thomas (later Bell) of Courtenay.

Hikers' Option: If you are going west to Flower Ridge by wa[...]zela Lake you now have a choice of routes (see map M6, page 40). I[...]re hikers rather than climbers and want to avoid any exposure and [...]f a rope for security, leave Rees Ridge at the 1780 m level and pick y[...] way down the steep southwest side, then down a small side ridge to[...] point near the outlet of Milla Lake, where there is a place to camp. Cross Shepherd Creek and contour around, a little below the 1230 m level, using open areas, then hike south up the glacier on the west side of Mount Harmston[43] (1980 m), keeping to the west side of the valley to stay clear of steep snow sections. This small glacier does not normally have any dangerous crevasses, but the ice has become more exposed. While it has receded a fair bit, the toe of the glacier is on relatively flat ground, and this may explain the stability. Keep to the right side near the top, over the pass and down to regain the main route at the snout of Cliffe Glacier.⑩

Climbers' Option: If you are climbers, and only if you are equipped and experienced, you may choose to follow down the ridge in a southeast direction from point ⑥ on the map. There are good campsites on the south-facing slope of this ridge.

From the col (saddle) below Rees Ridge, the escarpment looks very spectacular but the route is quite easy for experienced climbers, proving the truth of a well-known climber's advice: "you can't judge a mountain till you rub your nose on it" (the late Rex Gibson). On leaving the col, keep up the ridge to the small glacier, bearing right to follow the moraine between the snow and the top of cliffs above Moving Glacier where the route is exposed. This brings you to a steep gully across your path that runs from the base of the cliffs.⑦ Cross this near its top, using a rope for steep and exposed sections, contour slightly up and across the slope to the right for about 90 m, then climb straight up at the bottom of the cliff to a steep short gully which runs off to the right across the face. Follow this to its top, then climb up a short pitch and you are on the main ridge with Comox Glacier to your left and Argus Mountain to your right.

From the point where you gained the main ridge, follow a game trail over a small summit and down to the base of the northeast ridge of Argus Mountain[44]. Leave the ridge at this point and angle down across the snow slope on southeast side of Argus to the base of the south cliffs and contour

---

43. **Mount Harmston:** William Harmston, an early Comox Valley settler. Florence Cliffe, his daughter, had a son Lucius, for whom Cliffe Glacier is named.

44. **Argus Mountain:** Argus means "watchful guardian." Karl Stevenson, in his "Hiking in Strathcona Park" comments: "Mr. Ben Highes, editor of the Comox Argus, an early newspaper in the Comox Valley, tried to climb the mountain in 1931."

the south-facing scree slopes above the lower cliffs, working down the top of lower cliffs, then up again at about 1720 m. The first part the route around the cliff will be steep, exposed snow before July. It usually possible to go between the snow and the rocks at the base of the cliff. The route down off Argus Mountain onto Cliffe Glacier is easy if you pick the correct gully, near a small chimney.⑧ Where this gully opens out above a steep section, contour right, then down to the snow. Be cautious here, because where the glacier has melted back it leaves a hard sediment, which looks like sand but provides little purchase. Wear your crampons.

7.b Carey Lakes[45]   Map M7

DESCRIPTION The Carey Lakes plateau is a subalpine parkland with beautiful lakes and profuse blackberry picking in season. With the increased logging along the east side of the Cruickshank Valley, access to the Carey Lakes, and to Rees Ridge beyond has become feasible.

ACCESS From the causeway and dam at the foot of Comox Lake, take Comox Lake Main for 14.5 km to the Cruickshank River bridge. On the south side of the river, swing right, down to the river and follow Cruickshank Main approximately 3 km to where you get the most magnificent view of Comox Glacier. Point ㉟ on map M3. With Alone Mountain on your right, turn north on Cruickshank Main and climb through a logging "moonscape", angling westerly up the height of land north of Rees Creek and then switchbacking above the creek valley. Park near a small lake on your left, when the road begins to descend northward. It is about 2 km west to the Carey Lakes.

ROUTE From the end of the road, the hike runs through gently rolling terrain past small lakes, then either side of Carey Lakes, with good camping near the lakes or on the ridge above.

NOTE Climbers have used this route to access Rees Ridge via rough terrain along ridges west of the Lakes, then turning south above McQuillan Lake to join Rees Ridge.

---

45. **Carey Lakes**: Named for B.C.'s first Attorney General, who first recommended the Comox Valley for settlement, ca. 1865.

8

Della Falls

Access to this remote and beautiful region is via Great Central Lake, a 35 km long lake with steep mountain banks.

The Della Falls Trail leads hikers from the head of Great Central Lake to the base of Canada's highest falls (440 m), a cascade that tumbles down from Della Lake into Drinkwater[46] Creek. This 16 km trail, along Drinkwater Creek, is a long hike, about seven hours one way, suitable for intermediate level hikers.

In the valley below Della Falls a junction of several trails provides trail access to Love Lake to the north, a steep route southwest (44) beside the falls to gentle terrain around Della Lake, and a difficult valley route up the Drinkwater Creek Valley that connects eventually to Bedwell Lake.

8.a Drinkwater Creek   Map M8A (see also map M8)

DESCRIPTION The north and south shores of Great Central Lake are very precipitous, so if canoeing, kayaking or by small boat get an early morning start. The lake is usually windswept by west winds in mid-afternoon and the water can be very rough with whitecaps. Watch for deadheads and standing dead trees along the shore, due to the raising of the lake level. In case of rough water, follow the shoreline despite the hazards. There are a few possible campsites about halfway along the north shore. The Della Falls Trail up Drinkwater Creek starts at the head of Great Central Lake on the lake's northeast shore. Beware of avalanches in the winter and early spring. Following severe winters, lingering snows block the trail well into June in the upper valley. Flooding and high water may delay or prevent passage. The trail is seasonally overgrown and hard to find in some areas.

---

46. The trail was originally built by Joe Drinkwater, a trapper and area miner. He also started the Ark Resort. **Della Falls** is named after his wife.

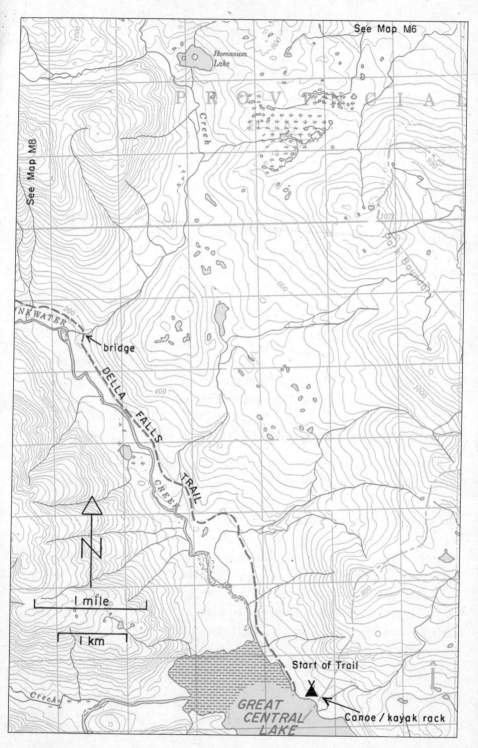

See Map M6

Homasum Lake

P R O V I N C I A L

See Map M8

Creek

Park Boundary

1071

600

600

1000

200

bridge

DELLA   FALLS

400

CREEK

TRAIL

N

1 mile

1 km

800

Start of Trail

Creek

GREAT CENTRAL LAKE

Canoe / kayak rack

Parts of the route up the Drinkwater Valley above Della Falls are extremely difficult. At the Della Falls trailhead BC Parks has developed a camping area with a bear-proof food cache, a pit toilet and a canoe/kayak/boat rack. Along the trail, all the suspension bridges have been replaced with timber bridges and a steel one. Much of the trail follows an old roadbed left behind from the days of logging and mining in the early 1900s.

ACCESS For Great Central Lake drive Highway 4 west from Port Alberni for just under 10 km and turn right (north) onto Great Central Lake Road. Continue another 7.5 km to the Ark Resort. You can park here for a small fee, and rent or launch a boat for your journey to the Della Falls trailhead at the head of Great Central Lake. Allow four days for a round trip to the Falls if using a powerboat and six days by canoe.

NOTE The Ark Resort rents out canoes, powerboats and kayaks. Ask for the Della Falls special rate, which includes a four-day canoe rental or a three-day power boat rental. You can also camp at the Ark Resort. They have ten campsites and nine RV sites. For information contact the resort at (250) 723-2657 or visit www.arkresort.com.

ACCESS A second lake access point is situated part way down the lake's north side. As above, drive to Great Central Lake and just before reaching the Ark Resort turn right (north) onto Island Timberland Ash River Main and cross the logging road bridge. These roads are administered by Island Timberlands. Call ahead to check on current access restrictions. (Appendix, page 215.)

After about 6.5 km turn left (west) onto Branch 83. Stay on Branch 83 for 9.3 km to a road intersection, south of Lowry Lake. Turn left (south) on a secondary spur and continue about 1.5 km to the BCFS Scout Beach Recreation Site and boat launch. Canoeing time to the head of the Great Central Lake is about four or five hours.

TRAIL The first 7 km follows the flats through a mixed second-growth forest to Margaret Creek (map M8A). Once across the bridge at this creek the trail continues through some old-growth forest for 4 km, gently gaining elevation. About 11 km up the valley a bridge over a scenic gorge crosses Drinkwater Creek. From there the trail gets rougher and climbs to a second bridge at the 12.5 km point. These spans are sometimes washed out, crushed or damaged by fallen trees. If creek traverses are necessary, try to cross at low water times and use poles or join hands to increase

Map M8 Della Falls

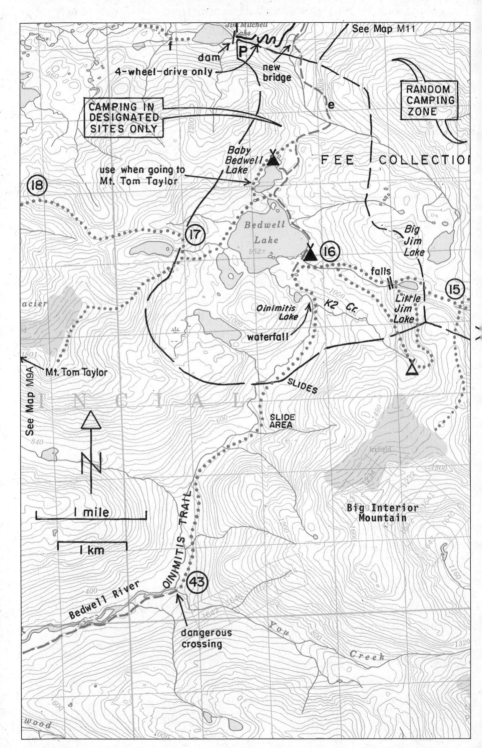

f

See Map M11

dam

4-wheel-drive only

P

new bridge

e

RANDOM CAMPING ZONE

CAMPING IN DESIGNATED SITES ONLY

FEE COLLECTION

use when going to Mt. Tom Taylor

Baby Bedwell Lake

Bedwell Lake
952

Big Jim Lake

16

falls

Little Jim Lake

15

18

17

acier

Oinimitis Lake

K2 Cr.

waterfall

See Map M9A

Mt. Tom Taylor

SLIDES

PROVINCIAL

SLIDE AREA

N

1 mile

1 km

OINIMITIS TRAIL

Big Interior Mountain

icefield

Bedwell River

43

dangerous crossing

You Creek

wood

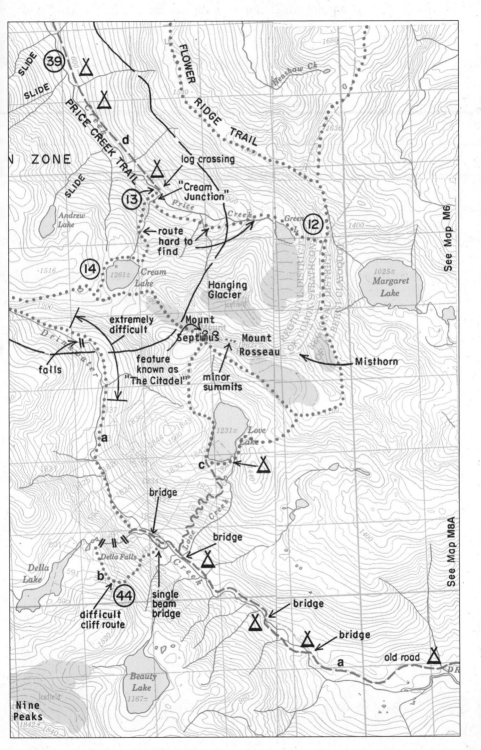

stability in moving water. Beyond the second crossing a challenging section of the route passes through a rockslide that pushes you close to the creek. Gaining elevation again, the trail leads up to the Love Lake Trail/ Mount Septimus[47] junction at about the 15 km mark. The last kilometre to Della Falls emerges from open old growth forest into an avalanche run-out zone near the base of the falls.

NOTES On the hike in, you can camp on the Drinkwater Creek gravel bar, about 2 km before the Love Lake turn-off. The building of campfires is prohibited in Strathcona Park's backcountry. Use a portable backpacking stove instead. Check maps M8 and M8A for campsites. BC Parks strongly advises visitors not to camp near the old sawmill site, about one kilometre below the falls. This area is surrounded by decadent forest (trees decaying and subject to blowdown) and is not suitable for camping. Instead find an alternate location along the creek's north side, dependent on water levels, that is not situated under any large or hazardous trees. When camping anywhere along Drinkwater Creek, be aware that the water can rise suddenly.

There is much evidence of the extensive mining activity in the Della Falls area. Please do not remove or destroy any remaining equipment or relics, which now form part of the historical record.

ROUTE From Della Falls it is possible to hike to the ridge between Cream Lake and Bedwell Lake. (See Section 8.d.) A difficult route, it initially crosses rocky slides north of the river following the true left bank, and this eventually turns north. Avoid bushy areas as much as possible, sometimes using bear trails to squeeze through the dense growth or by following the creek bed. As you angle west and climb steeply, stay right of the waterfall and then continue up to the ridge, often on remnant winter snow. Allow a very long day for this route.

8.b Della Lake, Nine Peaks   Map M8

DESCRIPTION Della Lake is a beautiful lake in a spectacular setting of rugged mountain peaks. To the south, Nine Peaks massif is arrayed on the horizon. Climbers can use this access to approach it from the north. Climbers also approach Nine Peaks over Big Interior Mountain, above

---

47. **Mount Septimus:** Septimus Evans was surgeon on the SS *Beaver*. By coincidence, the mountain has seven peaks.

Upper drop of Della Falls. Gil Parker

and to the west of Della Lake. Della Falls has three successive drops, each about 150 m in height. A climb from Drinkwater Valley to the top of the falls is possible but a little dangerous, especially if snow lingers near the top. Experienced climbers can tackle the difficult route that leads up the cliffs to the south of the falls.

ROUTE To get there, cross the Drinkwater Creek on the main bridge just above the upper campsite area. Walk 100 m and look for an overgrown trail to the left. The correct route crosses a single-beam bridge, 25 m after leaving the trail to the falls. The route takes you up through dense bush to the base of cliffs and then it follows obvious lines up through steep mixed ground with holds that are often tree roots. See photo, page 59. Above 800 m it leads up and right, (44) through bush, and connects to a ledge. This ledge leads up cliffs and straightforward ramps to Della Lake.

8.c Love Lake Map M8

DESCRIPTION Love Lake is a pristine lake in a cirque below the south face of Mount Septimus. The lake is on a route to Septimus and Flower Ridge around the east side of Mount Rosseau or west to Cream Lake. The climb from Drinkwater Valley to Love Lake is a steep switchback trail. Above the lake, the routes are best suited to experienced hikers or climbers. In early months of the summer, steep snow may be encountered, requiring ice axes and crampons.

TRAIL Map M8 shows the switchback trail, starting by the old sawmill site, which goes up to Love Lake. Turn uphill (right) at the sign "Love Lake/Mount Septimus." This is a well-built trail and a pleasant hike to good views of Della Falls. The best are at the 1200 m level, where you break off to the right and pick up the trail to Love Lake.

8.d Price Creek[48], Cream Lake Map M8 (also map M11)

NVI Mining Ltd (a subsidiary of Breakwater Resources Ltd) is now the owner of Boliden/Westmin Mine Area near Myra Falls. The mine site is about 40 km south of the Buttle Narrows bridge on Highway 28. At the head of Buttle Lake drive beyond the mine to the visitors' parking lot. Cars may be left here for the duration of the hike, but no camping is permitted in or around the parking lot. Until 4:00 pm, the company may be reached

---

48. **Price Creek** is named after the Hon. Price Ellison, who led a 1910 expedition up Campbell River to the present Strathcona Park, which he helped to create, in 1911.

Dave Green hikes vertical trail to Della Lake. GIL PARKER

at (250) 287-9271. Hikers may use the recreation building pay phone to arrange to be picked up. In the case of an emergency, the company office will help contact authorities to arrange helicopter evacuation.

DESCRIPTION The Price Creek Valley extends south from the head of Buttle Lake approximately 34.5 km south of the Buttle Narrows bridge on Highway 28 (or 8.5 km south of the Ralph River campsite). Turn off, left, just before the bridge over Price/Thelwood creeks. There are places along the creek to camp, but as the valley narrows there are avalanche chutes that are sometimes choked with snow, and in other seasons prone to Devil's Club overgrowth. The trail used to be the primary access to beautiful Cream Lake (named for its milky colour) which was also subject to extensive mining exploration. *BC Parks does not recommend the use of this access to Cream Lake. The preferred route is via the Bedwell Lake Trail.* (Section 8.e)

TRAIL The Price Creek Trail to Cream Lake is for strong hikers and gains 1000 m of elevation over 8.5 km and takes about seven hours one way, though most of this elevation gain occurs in the last 2 km. Members of the CDMC have relocated the upper part of this old elk trail, which provides difficult access to Cream Lake.

Hiker passes Cream Lake, Nine Peaks beyond.   GIL PARKER

The route stays on the east side of Price Creek right up to the Cream Creek Junction.(13) Here a log crosses Price Creek (with hand cable). The next arduous part of the route parallels the north side of Cream Creek up to about 275 m below Cream Lake, then crosses an open slide area up above the east side of the creek. The route is physically challenging, especially with a heavy pack, but not particularly technical. Route finding can be a dilemma since the avalanche zone can't be seen through the trees. Some forking in Cream Creek and a lot of blowdown in the forest roughly marks the location of the chute. Turn east to cross the creek and ascend the avalanche chute (in summer, of course) and head to a small snowfield above it and to the left. It is a short hike from the snowfield to Cream Lake.

The route skirts Cream Lake's north side and parallels the west shore.(14) If you climb to the ridge south of the lake, a great view of Nine Peaks and the upper part of Della Falls will appear.

Due to major impacts of camping in this area, there is a camping fee for the entire corridor from Price Creek to Cream Lake and out to the Bedwell Lake trailhead. Random camping is permitted along Price Creek and discouraged at Cream Lake. Camping fees are charged even though there are no facilities.

There are beautiful swimming ponds north of the lake even though there may still be ice in the main lake. Over-camping threatens this high alpine lake, and Parks prefers that you camp at Bedwell Lake. (See Section 8.e.) Above the lake a crescent snowfield descends from the west end of Mount Septimus, sometimes called "The Citadel."

8.e Bedwell Lake   Map M8 (also map M11)

DESCRIPTION Bedwell Lake and Baby Bedwell Lake are two areas in the centre of Strathcona Park that may be reached relatively easily along a well-used trail to beautiful lakes with prepared, hardened camping spots. This trail is now extremely popular and a significant impact on a sensitive and fragile area is the result. Visitors to the area can protect the wilderness qualities of this beautiful area by practising low impact techniques. The use of steel stairways on this trail continues to offend some hikers while being appreciated by others.

BC Parks has developed the Bedwell Lake Trail as an opportunity for less-experienced hikers to access an alpine/subalpine area. One of the best ways to see this area without further impacting it is to visit as a day hiker. With just a daypack, it is feasible to climb to the lake and return the same day.

BC Parks has designated the Bedwell Lake corridor as a core area within which campfires are banned. Camp stoves are required. At this altitude plants have a very short growing season and cannot recover from trampling. Soil cover in the alpine is thin and easily washed away if it is disturbed, for example, by trenching around tent sites. Restrict your hiking to marked trails. To lessen impact to the area, camping is allowed only at Bedwell and Baby Bedwell lakes. Camping fees are $5 per person over age 15, per night.

ACCESS To access the trailhead from the south end of Buttle Lake, leave the Buttle Lake Road (35 km from the Buttle Narrows bridge on Highway 28) and head for Jim Mitchell Lake (map M11 on page 78). Follow the signs about 6.8 km up a rough road (suitable for two wheel drive vehicles) to the trailhead information shelter and parking area.

NOTE There have been landslides along the road, so check that access is open before heading for this trailhead.

Due to major impacts of camping in this area, there is a camping fee for the entire corridor from Price Creek to Cream Lake and Bedwell Lake and its access trail. Random camping is permitted along Price Creek but is discouraged at Cream Lake. Campers here are subject to the camping fees even though facilities are not provided. Camping fees are $5 per person over age 15, per night (2008.) No fires are permitted.

TRAILS The trail is 6 km long, gains 600 m in elevation, and takes about three hours. It ascends a steep forested valley with numerous bridge crossings and then breaks out into a hilly subalpine area with two lakes and many tarns and creeks. There is designated camping at Baby Bedwell Lake, with 6 tent platforms and a pit toilet, and on the east shore of Bedwell Lake (16), where there are 10 tent platforms and a toilet.

BC Parks recommends the Bedwell Lake Trail for those hiking to Cream Lake. From Bedwell Lake climb east alongside the creek to the falls which drop from Little Jim Lake. Stay to the north of the lake and continue to the Drinkwater/Bedwell pass,(15) then along the ridge and down to Cream Lake. The route up from Della Falls via the Drinkwater Valley meets the ridge at the pass.

There is an optional route from Bedwell Lake to a valley on the north side of Big Interior Mountain where there are places one could camp. Head southeast from the main route contouring right to the head of K2

Creek, where there is a camping option. From here, you can hike north to the main route, joining it just above the falls.

Other side trips from Bedwell Lake include hikes up Mount Tom Taylor and Big Interior Mountain (1862 m), each requiring a full day. There is also a route from Bedwell Lake to Thelwood Mountain (18) which is described in Section 9.b, map M9A. This is part of an alternate route to Burman Lake.

The Oinimitis Trail down to the Bedwell River also begins at Bedwell Lake. See Section 9.a, page 64. This trail links with the Bedwell River Trail to form a through route between the Pacific Ocean (at Bedwell Sound) and Buttle Lake. There are many black bears in this area, and a management concept is being developed to prevent bear habitat from being disturbed by visitors.

8.f Thelwood Lake[49] via Jim Mitchell Lake
Map M8 (also map M11)

According to Karl Stevenson in his *Hiking in Strathcona Park*, in 1937, surveyors were camped near Thelwood Lake. They sent 17 year old Jim Mitchell for supplies. They later found his body downstream from a log crossing of Thelwood Creek. Jim Mitchell Lake was named for the boy.

ACCESS At the head of Buttle Lake, drive on the mine roads to the parking lot at the start of the Bedwell Lake Trail. Access from here to Jim Mitchell Lake (flooded 1985) is made either on foot or by four wheel drive vehicle only. A parking lot is provided just before Jim Mitchell Lake.

ROUTE There is no easy access from Jim Mitchell Lake dam to the Thelwood Lake area. It is advisable to take a canoe to the head of Jim Mitchell Lake then hike a rough bush route, made by mine employees, that follows the south side of the creek to Thelwood Lake. (There is also access to Upper Thelwood Lake from the Mount Thelwood area on the alternate route from Bedwell Lake to Burman Lake.) (See Sections 9 and 10.)

---

49. **Thelwood** Lake, Creek: Ethel Wood was wife of G. Cory Wood, MLA for Alberni, 1912-1914.

9

Bedwell Sound and River

What is now named the Bedwell River was the traditional home of the Oinimitis (meaning "bear") people, who, in the fall, would gather at the delta to fish and hunt. In 1865, John Buttle travelled up this river, climbing an unnamed mountain near Ursus Creek to discover Buttle Lake in the Island's interior. (Ursus is Latin for "bear".) He was soon followed by placer miners who swarmed here on the rumour of gold. Mining has continued in this valley since that time, and in 1962 the lower valley was partially logged. In the winter of 1994/95 the first 2 km of the old logging road were re-opened and an area of privately-owned timber was clearcut. The valley has been deleted from, and then returned to, Strathcona Park since 1986. The Oinimitis Trail was built by the Friends of Strathcona Park (FOSP) to provide access to this remote and delightful valley.

9.a Bedwell[50] River
Maps M9A, M9B (also map M8)

DESCRIPTION This trail provides part of a connection from Buttle Lake to the sea at Bedwell Sound. The link is completed by BC Parks' Bedwell Lake Trail that climbs up along Thelwood Creek (that runs into Buttle Lake). A through trip from Bedwell Sound to Bedwell Lake will take two to three days, with a further half day to reach the trailhead at Jim Mitchell Lake road. The Bedwell River Trail has received little maintenance or upgrading in recent years. The route is overgrown in places and difficult to find, particularly in the Ashwood Creek area and the lower valley where salmonberry and elderberry thrive, and many sections have eroded along the riverbank. The old road has washed out

50. **Bedwell** Lake, River, Sound: Captain Richards, commanding surveying vessels, named the Sound after Edward Parker Bedwell, second master of HM Surveying Vessel Plumper, 1857-1860.

in several spots and the decayed bridges are now completely gone. A flood event during 2006-7 caused major slides although the route is still passable by experienced hikers. Some areas may be treacherous in times of wet weather and high water.

This description will start at Bedwell Sound and proceed up river to Bedwell Lake. For continuation to Buttle Lake, see Section 8.e.

ACCESS From Tofino, boat or air transportation is needed to reach the head of Bedwell Sound, approximately 32 km. Travelling by sea kayak or canoe, this trip will take about a day and a half. Powerboat transportation can be arranged in Tofino and the trip takes about 1.5 hours.

TRAIL (Map M9B, page 66). The trail begins at an obvious, open flat area by the logging road bridge. Respect the private land in this area. There is a resort located here which does not provide supplies or services to hikers, but allows passage through their land. From the landing area, follow the logging road north, through 2 km of logged forest to reach the first camping site and fresh water, near the junction with Ursus Creek.

From this point the trail follows the true right bank of the Bedwell River and there are good views of Ursus Mountain. One kilometre farther on, cross Cotter Creek and then, just past Penny Creek, a small trail to the right leads to Walter Guppy's riverside cabin about 4 km from tidewater. This is a good shelter in bad weather. The main trail begins to climb a little and you reach the "3-Mile" log-crossing ㊵ where the trail crosses above a gorge on the Bedwell River. Here a fine suspension bridge has been constructed by the FOSP. In August, 1994, the FOSP dedicated this bridge to Gayle McGee, a departed Friend and an environmental activist. On the river's left bank, one kilometre north, you reach the unmarked boundary of Strathcona Park. The trail now opens up and stays well above the main river canyon. There are beautiful deep pools and water-carved rocks where the river bends (well below the trail) and a fine view of Mariner Mountain.

After the rock-cut, the trail becomes narrower, and after 500 m leads you to a rocky washout which can be tricky to cross. Shortly after this the Bedwell River is again crossed, this time via an overgrown bridge, high above a narrow canyon where the river roars far below. This is an interesting viewing point!

Continuing on Map M9A, page 68, follow the river's right bank, and approximately 800 m farther on, several flagging tapes on the left mark the beginning of the difficult route ㊶ to Mariner Mountain (1785 m), a steep route for experienced mountaineers, probably requiring ropes and

Map M9B   Bedwell Sound

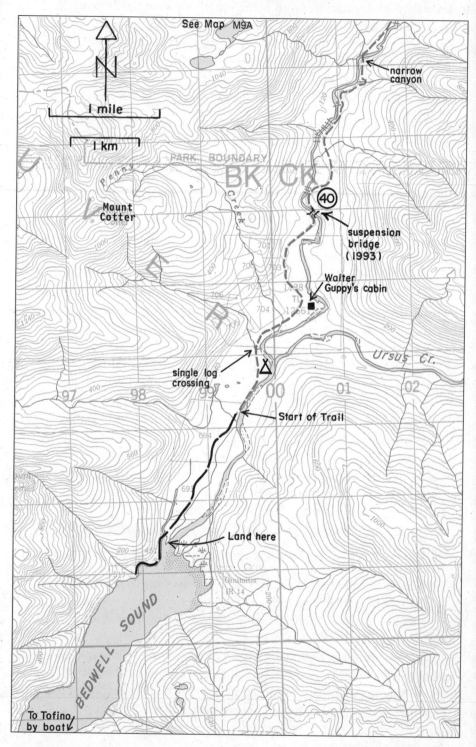

See Map M9A

narrow canyon

N
1 mile
1 km

PARK BOUNDARY

BK CK

Mount Cotter

Penny Creek

40

suspension bridge (1993)

Walter Guppy's cabin

single log crossing

Ursus Cr.

Start of Trail

Land here

Qinimitis IR 14

BEDWELL SOUND

To Tofino by boat

ice axes. Noble Creek is 200 m past this side trail, with possible camping sites. The crossing here is a dicey one across two fallen tree trunks. One kilometre past this creek there is an interesting side trip to see the "Twin Falls" and canyon. Small cairns on the right mark an easy bushwhack to this viewpoint.

About 5 km past Noble Creek the trail is forced closer to the river by big cliffs and crosses the Bedwell River for the last time at Ashwood Creek. (42) This is a very tricky ford of the river so be extra cautious. There is a spacious campsite a 10 minute walk up the trail along a dry creek bed that leads off to the left. This fine gravel bar campsite has an open view of the whole valley and Big Interior Mountain. The average hiker should reach this spot, about 14 km from tidewater, in about 5-8 hours.

On Map M8, page 54, on the south side (left bank) of the Bedwell River, you reach an old logging/mining road. Go no more than 45 m before swinging to the left. Otherwise you go in the wrong direction, well away from the river. The correct trail does cut away from the river for 1.5 km and then bypasses a 100 m washed-out section before rejoining the main route again. Another kilometre brings you to another potentially dangerous water crossing, (43) this time of You Creek[51]. There was an old bridge here, but it is now completely gone so you must ford the creek.

The old road continues for another 2 km up the valley, as it swings north and begins to climb more steeply. At the end of the old logging road the route follows a dry creek bed for a short section before turning off to the right (look for flagging tape) to reach the old-growth forest. It is difficult to locate the route in this area, up into the old-growth forest and through the slide areas. A recently scoured slide near the upper part of the valley makes this section extremely difficult. A series of old game trails, climbing steeply in sections, brings you into the slide areas by way of a small river crossing. Cairns mark the route across, climbing to reach the old-growth trees again. The trail winds through forest and swampy areas.

Shortly before K2 Creek a small side trail leads to an impressive waterfall, unofficially named "Doran Falls" after two brothers, Stan and George Doran, who rebuilt this section of trail when well into their 70s. A rustic bridge atop a waterfall leads over K2 Creek. The route climbs to a side trail going to Oinimitis Lake and in half an hour, through fragile alpine meadows, you reach Bedwell Lake.

The BC Parks trail out to Thelwood Creek, and thus to Buttle Lake, starts at the campsite at the southeast corner of Bedwell Lake.

---

51. **You Creek** was named by Norm Stewart after the You Mineral Claim.

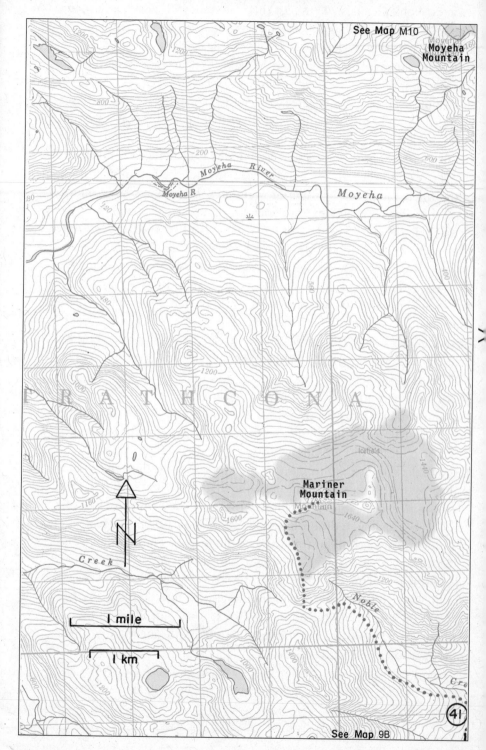

See Map M10

Moyeha Mountain

Moyeha River

Moyeha R

Moyeha

STRATHCONA

Mariner Mountain

Icefield

Creek

Noble

1 mile

1 km

41

See Map 9B

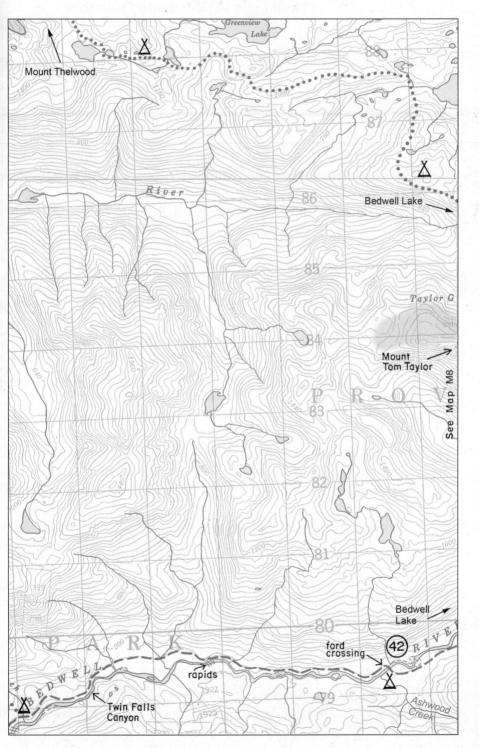

Mount Thelwood

Greenview Lake

88

River

87

Bedwell Lake

86

85

Taylor G

84

Mount Tom Taylor

See Map M8

P   R   O   V

83

82

81

Bedwell Lake

80

ford crossing

(42)

RIVE

P   A   R   K

rapids

BEDWELL

Twin Falls Canyon

79

Ashwood Creek

9.b Bedwell Lake to Thelwood Mountain
Map M9A (also maps M8 and M10)

DESCRIPTION This is a multi-day mountain-hiking route, requiring experience in navigating in the backcountry, using map, compass and perhaps a GPS. This section of the route is characterized by glaciated granite, with many hidden drops, which must be circumnavigated. This section may be linked with other routes north of Thelwood Lake, to join with Phillips Ridge and eventually, reach Burman Lake.

TRAILS (Map M8, page 54) From the camping area at Bedwell Lake, go north on the main trail and gain the route around Bedwell Lake by crossing the outfall of Baby Bedwell Lake. Stay close to the lake shore, and after crossing a stream at the most westerly point of the lake turn west and ascend a moderate slope to about the 1100 m level. From here, the route to the summit of Mount Tom Taylor (1801 m) continues southwest up a prominent ridge. The cross-country route to Thelwood Mountain turns north, crossing a creek ⑰ just below its lake outlet and bluff. Ascend the small side ridge north of this lake and head up to the Bedwell/Moyeha pass, then travel northwest following the centre of a ridge for about 800 m.

A steep section leads down about 220 m to a very attractive camping area ⑱ looking across to the Taylor Glacier. Referring to Map M9A, page 68, continue north by way of a flat open ridge to the lake on the Moyeha River drainage south of Thelwood Lake, bear left at a steep section near the bottom and cross the creek a short way below the outlet. This is the lowest elevation (850 m) on this route. Here, in the western section of the park, north-facing slopes and level areas are open heather due to heavy winter snowfall. South-facing slopes can be bushy (rhododendron) to the 1080 m level.

From the valley floor hike west up the centre of the ridge lying south of Greenview Lake, which is bushy and a little hard to get onto at the lower level, but well-defined and clear going above 950 m. The hump south of Greenview Lake can be contoured around on its southwest side at the 1080 m level, then up into a beautiful, hanging valley with arrowhead-shaped lakes and good camping areas. Continue west past the lakes and swing up to the saddle on the east ridge of Moyeha Mountain (1794 m), and down the other side in a north-west direction to about the 1100 m level.

Continuing on Map M10 page 75, at map point ⑲ you have a choice: around Mount Thelwood (1731 m) on its east side, or over it. For the route around, drop down and cross the creek (open going) then head north up the gully and open slope west of the main creek leading to the little "square" lake east of Mount Thelwood. This section makes for very difficult going when there is no snowpack. The east side of the creek is no better. Pass the "square" lake ⑳ and go on through the meadows, dropping down to about 1230 m, then contour around on game trail under the cliffs—not too low—to reach heather meadows north of Mount Thelwood.

For a side trip, well worth the effort, go down Thelwood Creek to Upper Thelwood Lake and the beautiful flower meadows there.

For the route over Mount Thelwood, contour left into the pass at base of southwest ridge, then straight up this ridge to the summit. A route east from here descends to map point ⑳ and bypasses the sometimes-difficult route around Mount Thelwood. From the summit, hike north across snowfield and down to the heather meadows. It is a good route if you have the energy and weather is clear.

For a continuation of this route to Phillips Ridge, see the next section.

The Red Pillar and Argus Mountain from the north.   JOHN GIBSON

10

Mount Thelwood

10.a Mount Thelwood to Phillips Ridge Map M10

DESCRIPTION While not a heavily used area, Mount Thelwood is the focus of several alpine routes. There are side access routes down to Tennent Lake and Upper Myra Falls. (See Section 11.) Descriptions in this section will continue the route from Bedwell Lake to Phillips Ridge, started in Section 9.b.

TRAILS From the meadows north of Mount Thelwood, go north and a little to the east, crossing the low point of an alpine ridge northeast of Thelwood that divides the north and south branches of Myra Creek.㉑

From map point ㉑ drop down 30 m or so, then contour left at about the 1140 m level, up to left of a round hump and a little lake, then north to open slopes leading to the west. Contour around at this level and up to the ridge near the lakes to join the alternate route, described next.

The alternate route to this point, from the heather meadows north of Mount Thelwood, involves more climbing and takes you higher than the above. Hike west from these meadows and through a pass to an attractive meadow at the head of Bancroft Creek.㉒ From the northeast side of this meadow turn north and go up, past a steep area on the right, then east to the 1600 m level. Descend the north ridge and swing right after passing lakes below you on the east side, joining the main route described above.

The route trends generally northwards down a steep section to the outlet of a lake which is part of the Burman River watershed. There are camping options at the lake outlet. Continue north into the timber and contour to the right at 1020 m, then up through bush to the head of larger Harvey Lake from which issues the north fork of Myra Creek eastward. A less bushy route goes east, up the centre of a ridge ㉓ to the west end of

Harvey Lake, then down to a heather meadow. This involves about 300 m of climbing, but is well worth it if the bushes are wet.

Head north around west end of Harvey Lake and climb a 30 m steep section, staying a little to the right. When open alpine is reached, continue north up a gradual slope and past a small lake near the ridge centre, then east along the centre of the ridge to the west peak of Phillips Ridge. Bear right at the steep parts of the lower levels.(24) Halfway up the ridge, the route leaves an area of glaciated granite. East of this peak turn north and descend a limestone ridge. This is the Phillips Ridge route, commonly followed north from the Myra Creek mine and which is described in Section 13.b.

Hiker at tarn on ridge above Arnica Lake. GIL PARKER

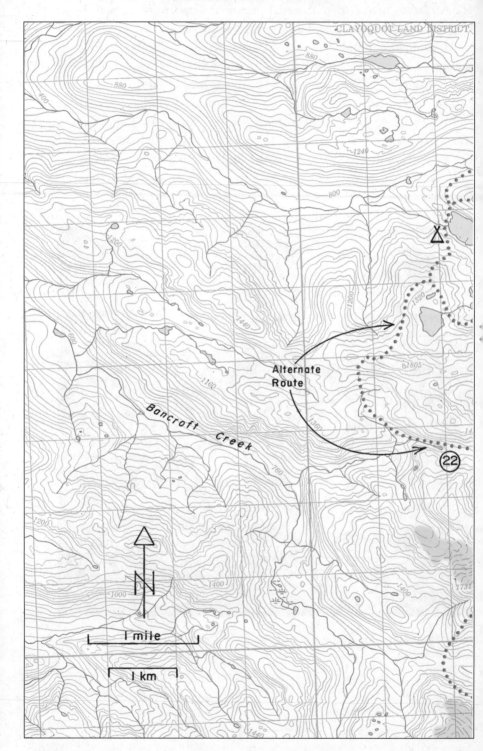

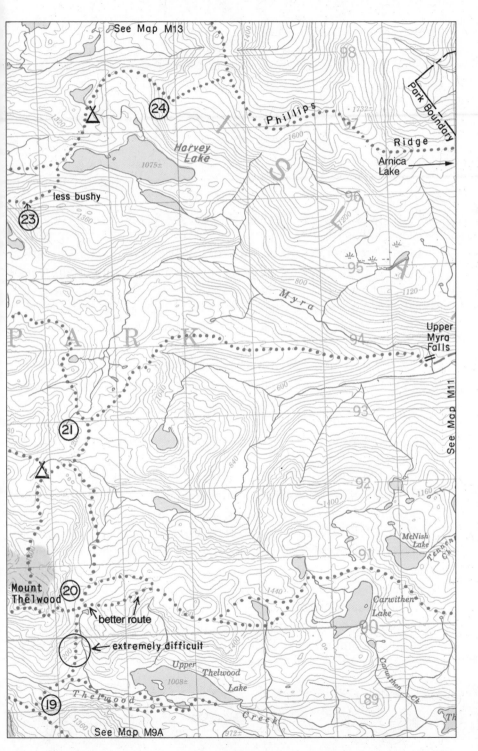

See Map M13

24

Harvey
Lake

1075±

Phillips

Ridge

1732

Arnica
Lake

98

less bushy

23

96

95

1120

Myra

Upper
Myra
Falls

P   A   R   K

94

600

See Map M11

93

21

92

1160

91

McNish
Lake

Tennent Ck

Mount
Thelwood

20

better route

extremely difficult

1440

Carwithen
Lake

90

Upper
Thelwood
Lake

1008±

Carwithen Ck

89

Thelwood

19

Creek

972±

11

South Buttle Lake

Buttle Lake was named after John Buttle, a member of the Vancouver Island Exploration Expedition of 1864, and leader of a group who, in 1865, discovered this 32 km long, narrow lake running north-south in the interior of Vancouver Island. The lake provides important marine and road access into the central area of Strathcona Park. The paved Buttle Lake (Parkway) Road, which follows the east shore, leaves Highway 28 (the Gold River highway) at the Buttle Narrows bridge. This is 47.7 km west of the junction of Highways 19 and 28, near Campbell River. The Parkway runs south to end at the major mine site near Myra Creek.

Along the west side of Buttle Lake are arrayed many beautiful mountains. A few kilometres south of the narrows and the bridge to Gold River, you can see Mount Haig-Brown (1948 m) directly north of Mount Con Reid (1744 m). It is named after Campbell River's well-known writer, the late Roderick Haig-Brown.

NVI Mining Ltd (a subsidiary of Breakwater Resources Ltd) is now the owner of Boliden/Westmin Mine Area near Myra Falls. At the head of Buttle Lake continue beyond the mine to the visitors' parking lot. Cars may be left here for the duration of the hike, but no camping is permitted in or around the parking lot. Until 4:00 pm, NVI Mining may be reached at (250) 287-9271. Hikers may use the recreation building pay phone to arrange to be picked up. In the case of an emergency, the company office will help contact authorities.

Camping fees apply at various Buttle Lake marine campsites and one on Upper Campbell Lake. Backcountry camping fees apply to Price Creek, the Bedwell Lakes and the ridge between.

11.a Upper Myra Falls to Thelwood Meadows
Map M11 (See also Map M10)

TRAIL From the parking area past the mine, walk past the gate on a gravel road about 800 m, and turn right where the trail cuts into the bank on the right. Follow the markers on a valley walk through mature timber. At the end of the trail by the falls, BC Parks has built a lookout platform. It is about an hour to the falls.

NOTE As part of the Adopt-A-Trail program organized by the Federation of Mountain Clubs of BC, this trail and its maintenance was formally adopted in 1991 by CDMC as the first such project on Vancouver Island.

TRAIL There is a flagged route (by CDMC) that provides direct access beyond the Falls and up to the Thelwood area. Follow the Upper Myra[52] Falls trail, just past an area of blowdown where the trail turns southwards, downhill, to a fork in the creek. Referring to Map M10, cross the creek—somewhat difficult in spring when water levels are high—and climb up the centre of a ridge due west and then southwest to reach the meadows north of Mount Thelwood.(21) The ridge is dry, so carry enough water to reach alpine areas where water may be found.

11.b Tennent Lake, Mounts Myra and Thelwood
Map M11 (See also map M10)

DESCRIPTION Mount Myra offers spectacular views of all the high peaks in the southern end of Strathcona Park. The trail up Mount Myra via Tennent Lake takes about 5 hours up and 3.5 down.

TRAILS Hike from the parking lot above the mine along the road to the powerhouse on Tennent Creek; follow the penstock road up to Tennent Lake (very rough and steep). It is about one hour to the lake. At Tennent Lake take the well-cairned trail from the south end of the small concrete retaining walls.

From here, the trail climbs towards the west side of Mount Myra (1814 m), passing tarns and tree copses (1 hour) before climbing a steep

---

52. **Myra** Falls, Creek and Mountain: For Myra Ellison, named by her father, Price Ellison, after their 1910 exploratory trip, or possibly for Myra Cliffe, daughter of Samuel Cliffe, a Comox pioneer.

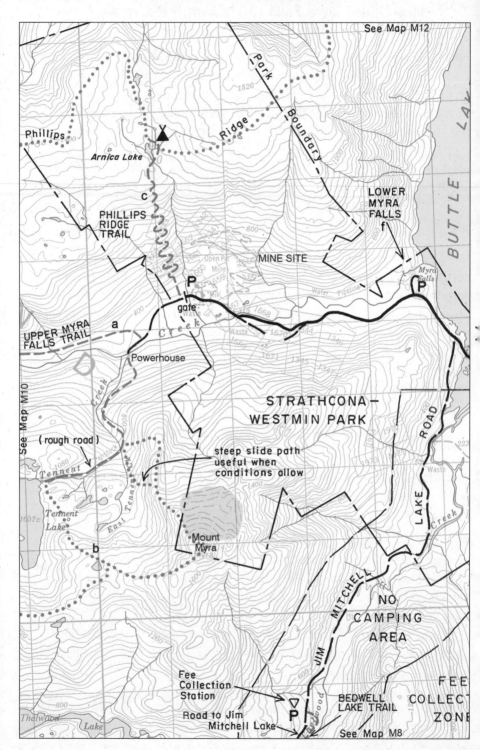

See Map M12

Phillips

Arnica Lake

Park Ridge

Boundary

c

LOWER
MYRA
FALLS
f

PHILLIPS
RIDGE
TRAIL

MINE SITE

BUTTLE LAKE

Myra
Falls

P

P

gate

UPPER MYRA
FALLS TRAIL

a

Creek

Powerhouse

STRATHCONA–
WESTMIN PARK

LAKE ROAD

See Map M10

(rough road)

Tennent

steep slide path
useful when
conditions allow

Tennent
Lake

East Tennent

Mount
Myra

NO
CAMPING
AREA

b

MITCHELL

JIM

FEE
COLLECT
ZONE

Fee
Collection
Station

Road to Jim
Mitchell Lake

P

BEDWELL
LAKE TRAIL

Thelwood
Lake

See Map M8

bluff up an often wet gully, that brings you onto an upper flank of Mount Myra. Follow the trail (or over large snow patches, even in late summer) gradually reaching the spine of the ridge and then moving onto its south side. Near the top of the ridge, the summit is blocked by steep bluffs. The trail goes straight up the middle on a steep but safe track. Inexperienced hikers may like a rope here.

Two alternate routes to the top of Mount Myra start along the old road near East Tennent Creek and climb directly to the northwest ridge.

You can reach Mount Thelwood from Tennent Lake. As you climb southeast on the lower ridge above Tennent Lake, you will reach a tarn (small mountain lake) that marks the start of a route to Mount Thelwood. Turn right above the tarn and contour southeast on open terrain between McNish and Carwithen lakes. Eventually, the route reaches the route from Bedwell Lake to Thelwood in meadows north of the peak or at a small lake east of the mountain.

11.c Myra Creek to Phillips Ridge   Map M11

DESCRIPTION This well-constructed trail affords access to the high ridge tour of the Phillips Ridge watershed without the need to cross Buttle Lake by boat. It is also the most popular starting point for the route to the Golden Hinde, and for continuation to the Elk River Valley. (See Sections 13.b, 14.a and 15.a)

This trail was initiated by the Comox District Mountaineering Club (CDMC) and has been a joint project of BC Parks and the Federation of Mountain Clubs of BC. Upgrades are done mainly by CDMC and Island Mountain Ramblers (IMR) volunteers. While the steep, switchback trail is clearly defined, the ridges to the north and east on Phillips Ridge are backcountry routes, requiring skill with compass and map reading, (and possibly GPS) and experience in multi-day backpacking.

TRAIL Drive through the mine site to the parking area, then walk about 30 m past the yellow gate on the gravel road and turn right at the BC Parks sign. The trail starts at the 360 m level and switchbacks up to the 1200 m level. It passes through open woods up to Arnica Lake[53] and then enters alpine meadows and ridges.

Hiking time to Arnica Lake, 3 to 4 hours; with large packs, four to five hours. First available water is at 460 m, a few minutes past the waterfalls;

---

53. **Mountain Arnica** (*arnica latifolia*), with bright yellow daisy-like flowers is found at higher elevations.

the second water is at 730 m; and then at Arnica Lake, 1200 m. Areas around the lake and the shoulders of Mount Phillips have beautiful seasonal flowers. This is a fairly strenuous day hike.

NOTES Hikers are now directed around the east side of the Arnica Lake only, and the old camp and trails are now a reclamation area. Fire pits have been eradicated. Five tent platforms have been installed at a dedicated campsite and a boardwalk provides lakeshore access. BC Parks has installed a pit toilet and a bear-proof cache at the northeast side of the lake, not far from the campsite. In order to help protect this area from unintentional abuse, BC Parks has erected an educational sign describing ethics for backcountry users.

11.d Flower Ridge   Map M11 (also map M8)

DESCRIPTION This is a steep, rough and dry trail up from Buttle Lake direct to the alpine. While it is best suited to experienced hikers, at least there is an easy to follow trail. After the first hour there are side trails which lead to viewpoints overlooking Buttle Lake. Once the alpine is

Flower Ridge and Buttle Lake from Mount Septimus.   GIL PARKER

reached, a burn area and sparse timber allows good views of Mount Myra, Mount Septimus and distant views of other mountains of Strathcona Park. This can make a good, if strenuous, day hike.

The walk along the ridge top of Flower Ridge is a perfect example of the appeal of clear alpine ridges. With views in all directions and many tarns beside which to camp, the ridge itself is a valid objective, one that keeps you coming back. In addition, there are other connections to Flower Ridge, most of them for experienced mountaineers.

TRAILS The trailhead is just south of the Henshaw[54] Creek bridge, about 3.5 km south of Ralph River campsite, sign-posted in the parking lot by Henshaw Creek. Elevation gain up to the ridge is about 1160 m, over about 6 km. The first part of the trail is well-defined through beautiful, open woods. The trail becomes very steep in places because the trail lacks switchbacks, but the views become progressively better as you climb. Time up, 4 or 5 hours; down, 3 hours. To reach the alpine area at the top of the ridge where you get the best views and where there are some ponds to camp beside, allow plenty of daylight hours.

At the south end of Flower Ridge (map M8, page 54) the route from Tzela Lake joins from the north. (See Section 6.d, page 43.) From this junction, one can continue to drop to the south, to the saddle between Price Creek and Margaret Lake.(12) To continue around Mount Rosseau and Misthorn follow the ridge about one kilometre and contour around to the south side of Mount Rosseau[55] staying below the remnants of glaciers and snowfields. From here, hikers may descend a good route to Love Lake and to the base of Della Falls, or contour west across the south face of Mounts Rosseau and Septimus and descend a snowfield to Cream Lake.

From that same point of departure (12) (on map M8) hikers may continue down the Price Creek Valley, taking advantage of clear areas at the lower end of slides as much as possible to avoid the thick tangle of vegetation. This is a difficult route to find, especially as conditions change from year to year. Below Green Lake, cross to the true left side of Price Creek and follow it down to Cream Creek.(13) At this point one can join the climb up to Cream Lake or exit down Price Creek.

---

54. **Henshaw Creek:** The name appears on a 1913 map; Henshaw may have been a prospector.
55. **Mount Rosseau:** Ralph Rosseau, a local mountaineer, killed in 1954 climbing Mount Septimus.

Experienced and equipped mountaineers may climb to the summit of Mount Rosseau and avoid the traverse around Misthorn. Similarly, there are routes across the north face of Mount Septimus, which allow climbers to contour west, either above or below Green Lake, and using slides and game trails, to reach Cream Lake. These routes involve dangers from rock and icefall and are not recommended for hikers.

11.e Shepherd[56] and Henshaw Watershed
Map M11 (also map M6)

DESCRIPTION There are several variations on the ridge routes on the east side of Buttle Lake. These can be used for access to the lakes and ridges near Rees Ridge, (See Section 7) or, in bad weather, can be used as exit routes from the high country.

The route up the ridge between Shepherd and Henshaw Creeks leaves the Buttle Lake road just north of Henshaw Creek, about 3.5 km south of the Ralph River campground. This is *not* Shepherd Creek Rescue Route that only follows Shepherd Creek about 5 km.

TRAIL Hike due east through dense forest to a more open area under some mature forest. Staying on the south side of Shepherd Creek, continue south-east up to the centre of the ridge. It is clear going under old-growth forest up to the alpine zone, but keep clear of an old burn near Shepherd Creek.

The summit ridge involves some climbing, but this can be avoided, given safe conditions, by contouring across the snow slope to the glacier. After the summit, contour across glaciers to pass north of Tzela Lake.

An alternative route avoids snow slopes but adds some steep hiking. It leaves the main route, contouring left at map point ㊲ to pass above small lakes, then climbs to regain the main route at point ㊳ map M6, page 40.

11.f Lower Myra Falls   Map M11

One kilometre beyond Thelwood Creek bridge at the south end of Buttle Lake turn right onto a gravel road leading to a signed parking area, and follow a gentle walking trail down to Myra Falls. This one-kilometre walk takes 20-40 minutes and features old-growth forest and a good view of these impressive multiple falls.

---

56. **Shepherd Creek:** F.H. Shepherd surveyed the E&N Railway in 1909.

12

Central Buttle Lake

12.a Ralph River[57] to Rees Ridge
Map M12 (also map M7)

TRAIL The Ralph River Route leaves the Buttle Lake road at the north end of the Ralph River bridge. Cross a log jam at the junction of Shepherd Creek and Ralph River. The next section is bushy through a burn and the forest here is almost impenetrable, thick hemlock. Keep within the sound of Shepherd Creek until you reach unburned timber, then angle back to the left, staying in old-growth as much as possible until past the burn. Near the timberline, bear right to avoid cliffs.

Continuing on Map M7, this alternate route to Rees Ridge leads up to the ridge above Delight Lake. Cross the triangular glacier north of Ink Lake and up its east side to gain the main ridge ⑤ and the route from Mount Albert Edward to Rees Ridge and the Comox glacier. (Section 7.a)

12.b Shepherd Creek Loop   Map M12

TRAILS Shepherd Creek Loop Trail is located directly across Buttle Lake Road from the BC Parks Ralph River campground, about 26 km south of the Buttle Narrows bridge. This interesting one-kilometre nature walk features a Pacific dogwood tree and a marshy area. Start just south of the Ralph River bridge. For its first 200 m the trail follows the bank of the creek, and it has an overall elevation gain of 50 m.

Wild Ginger Loop is a shorter walking trail located just north of the Ralph River bridge.

Shepherd Creek Rescue Route: Hikers on the high ridges east of Buttle Lake have few routes to follow when escaping bad weather. (See also map

---

57. **Ralph River:** William Ralph surveyed the western boundary of the E&N Railway Land Grant (later the east boundary of Strathcona Park) in 1892.

M11.) This rescue trail was worked on by hiking club volunteers in order to provide some help to those trying to drop down to Buttle Lake and the highway near the Shepherd Creek Loop Trail. A thick growth of small hemlocks impedes some lower stretches of the route. The route continues up the south side of Shepherd Creek approximately 5 km.

12.c Karst Creek Loop Map M12

The trail, around 23 km south of the Buttle Narrows bridge, is suitable for all ages and is signposted at the Karst Creek day-use area. Here there is swimming, picnicking and a boat launch. The latter used to be called the Ralph River Boat Ramp. The creek disappears into limestone and the 45 minute loop trail returns along the beautiful valley floor.

12.d Augerpoint Fire Loop Map M12

This trail, suitable for all ages, is a 15-20 minute walk through an area burned during the Augerpoint fire, instructional for that reason. The trail starts from the picnic area, just over a kilometre south of Jack's Augerpoint Trail.

12.e Augerpoint to Mount Albert Edward
Map M12 (also map M2)

DESCRIPTION This trail is a steep, switchback trail that leads directly to the alpine zone east of Buttle Lake, and is part of a traverse of the eastern part of Strathcona Park to the Mount Washington trailhead via Mount Albert Edward. (See Section 2.d and map M2.)

ACCESS The trail is located off the Buttle Lake (Parkway) Road about 20.5 km south of the Highway 28 junction at the Buttle Narrows bridge (or 2.4 km if going north from Karst Creek boat ramp.) Look for roadside parking. The old Augerpoint Trail was burned out in a forest fire and is still unusable, but Jack Shark, a member of CDMC, constructed a trail that goes up north of the burn. The start of this unofficial trail is 550 m north of the old trail and is flagged, but not signposted except for a red line on the highway.

TRAIL In about two hours you reach a little pond where you can camp, and three hours beyond the pond, at the 1400 m level, the trail breaks out into the sub-alpine of a pleasant plateau with small ponds and good camping opportunities. The trail turns southeast for a half mile to link up with the old trail; this section has now been slashed out and marked.

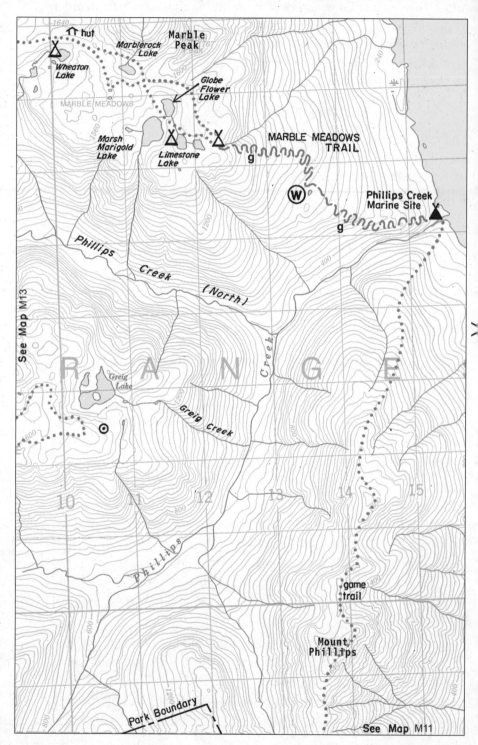

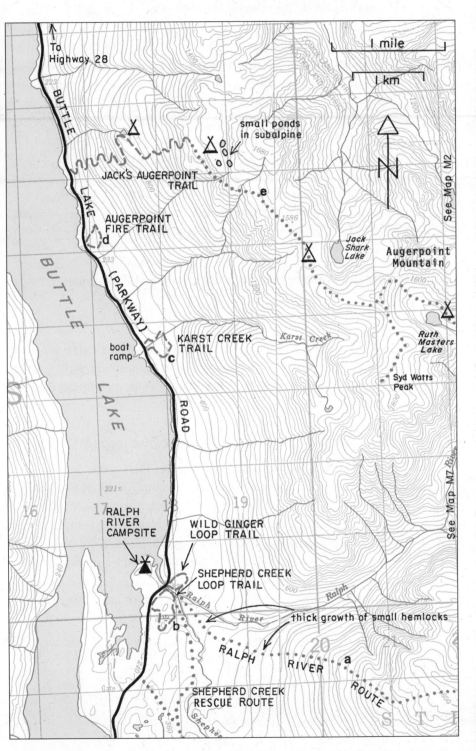

To Highway 28

BUTTLE LAKE (PARKWAY) ROAD

BUTTLE LAKE

1 mile

1 km

N

See Map M2

small ponds in subalpine

JACK'S AUGERPOINT TRAIL

AUGERPOINT FIRE TRAIL

d

e

Jack Shark Lake

Augerpoint Mountain

KARST CREEK TRAIL

boat ramp

c

Karst Creek

Ruth Masters Lake

Syd Watts Peak

16   17   18   19   20

221±

RALPH RIVER CAMPSITE

WILD GINGER LOOP TRAIL

SHEPHERD CREEK LOOP TRAIL

Ralph

River

thick growth of small hemlocks

b

RALPH RIVER ROUTE

a

SHEPHERD CREEK RESCUE ROUTE

Shepherd

Gate

See Map M7 Ralph River

If travelling west from Ruth Masters[58] Lake, do not go down the old trail to Buttle Lake, which seems nice at the start but will drop you into the burned area. Continue north for one kilometre to the area of small ponds and descend from there on a steep trail.

If travelling east towards Mount Albert Edward, follow cairns along the sometimes hard-to-locate route until you come to the foot of the southwest ridge of that mountain. There is only one place to get up, staying as far to the right (south) as possible. Of course, if you are hiking westward, go down the ridge staying on the south side.

NOTES There is an 853 m elevation advantage if you hike this route westward from Paradise Meadows to Buttle Lake. This alpine area has several options for camping, either above Jack Shark Lake or near Ruth Masters Lake. Above the latter a route continues south to Syd Watts[59] Peak. All three features are named for these pioneer explorers. Watts and Masters have long been contributors to these hiking guides.

12.f Lupin Falls

While not shown on our maps, this trail is signposted about 8 km south of the Buttle Narrows bridge. A 20-minute loop nature walk through an open "big tree" forest brings you to Lupin Falls. At lakeside there are picnic tables and beach access.

12.g Marble Meadows   Map M12 (also maps M13, M11)

DESCRIPTION This popular route requires boat access across Buttle Lake. The hike to the alpine is on a trail that climbs directly to a group of lakes and a mountain hut. From this point onward, it is a route as opposed to a trail. The Marble Meadows route provides access for climbers to Mount McBride, Morrison Spire, and joins the route from Myra Creek mine to the Golden Hinde. Along the way, a side route continues to Greig Ridge above Greig Lake. It is also possible to complete the loop back to the outlet of Phillips Creek by continuing south and then east along

---

58. **Ruth Masters** is a trail maker, place namer, and conservationist who has contributed widely to the preservation of wilderness. She writes, "Ruth Masters Lake and Syd Watts Peak are lined up… to become official two years after Syd and I go upstairs."
59. **Syd Watts** is a hiker/climber/naturalist who has developed many of the backcountry routes in this book, and has described them for future wilderness travellers.

Phillips Ridge past Arnica Lake (map M11), climbing Mount Phillips and descending the long north ridge to the creek outlet.

ACCESS From the Buttle Narrows bridge drive south about 23 km to the Karst Creek boat ramp if using a boat, or to the Augerpoint picnic area (to the north) if using a canoe. After crossing the lake, when landing at BC Parks' Marine Site at Phillips Creek, watch for underwater stumps.

TRAIL The trail starts on the north side of the creek and is well graded to a creek and camping spot. The trail then becomes steep and it switchbacks up to alpine meadows. This trail was constructed as a Centennial project by IMR and CDMC with the help of BC Parks. There are camping options in the area of Limestone Lake and at Wheaton Lake. Time up to the Wheaton Hut area is about 5 hours (some groups with heavy packs require 7 hours). This hut is very small and there are no toilets. Hikers should depend on using tents and practise no-trace camping.

The direct route to the southwest ridge of Marble Peak bears a little right from a cairn, through a limestone section, and no height is lost. Cross the upper meadows by a good game trail to a col west of Marble Peak (1768 m). By following this route, hiking traffic is directed away from the flower meadows around the lakes, already showing damage from over-use. From this col there is a choice of routes to the area of the Wheaton Hut. See map M12.

Continue down, past the hut, up the next slope a short way and contour west at about the 1540 m level, above Wheaton Lake at the head of the north fork of Phillips Creek. A wide fault leads west to a 1600 m elevation ridge. Aiming for point (31), the prominent Morrison Spire dominates the immediate western skyline. (See map M13.) See Section 13.a for the continuation to Phillips Ridge.

To climb Mount McBride (2081 m) to the north from here, allow 12 hours return.

13

Golden Hinde

13.a Marble Meadows to Mount Phillips

Map M13 (also maps M12, M10)

DESCRIPTION A continuation of the loop around the Phillips Creek watershed, this route is one of the most direct for access to the alpine in Strathcona Park. This description takes you from the Marble Meadows[60] area, southwest to Burman Lake and the Golden Hinde region, then south and east past Arnica Lake over Mount Phillips, and finally, connects to Section 11.c for the descent to Myra Creek near Buttle Lake.

TRAIL Follow the ridge centre to a col below a waterfall coming off the main north-south ridge from Mount McBride. Contour at 1540 m level around the last bump. Go up to 1620 m, then turn south along an exposed limestone fault (with fossils) and follow this line into the col north of Limestone Cap, where there is a good campsite if needed. From here, or even earlier, it is worth your while to hike to the summit of Morrison Spire, which is easy from the back (southwest) side. Limestone Cap is a flat-topped rock escarpment, deeply fissured through rainwater erosion—a fascinating place to explore. Its south slope is deep with wildflowers in spring.

The route then follows the divide south and is straightforward to a small, flat, east-west ridge,(32) just north of an 1820 m bump. This ridge has a cliff on its south side, not shown on the NTS map, which can be avoided by contouring into the col, following an exposed ledge and gully around the west side. There are three ledges, but the one you need goes

60. **Marble Meadows:** Named for the limestone (marble) formations in the region.

right down to the col, with a short drop at the end, where packs must be handed down—easy to find going south to north.

Continue south to the 1820 m summit, which can be avoided by traversing its east side, low down. Descend, keeping to the clear ground east of the ridge's centre, ③③ to a large col north of Greig[61] Ridge. Go up from this col to a good campsite at the west end of Greig Ridge. There is an easy side trip east along Greig Ridge to see the alpine flowers. The main route around the watershed continues southwest, left around a steep section near a summit and on down to a col ㉕ to meet with the Bedwell to Burman route. (See Section 13.b for the descent to Burman Lake and route north to Elk River.)

Continue south, passing the junction with the route from the southwest, Bedwell Lake and Mount Thelwood, then hike to the west peak of Phillips Ridge and head southeast. Briefly on map M11 on page 78, follow the ridge east around the south side of the Phillips Creek watershed. Continue east on the circuit to Mount Phillips. (The trail down to the Myra Creek mine site leaves the plateau at Arnica Lake; see Section 11.c, page 80.)

On map M12, hike over Mount Phillips (1723 m) and along the narrow north ridge. Go over the north summit (1684 m) and keep to the north ridge. At a point where the ridge becomes broken, follow a good game trail at the top of the meadows on the east side. Continue north, leaving this game trail when it veers east. At the 1230 m level take the right-hand ridge, leading down to Buttle Lake at Phillips Creek.

13.b Phillips Ridge to Burman Lake
Map M13 (also maps M10, M11)

DESCRIPTION This description starts at Arnica Lake above the Myra Creek mine site, see Section 11.c, and guides you to Burman Lake, below Golden Hinde. The terrain is typical of backcountry Strathcona Park, where you must be self-reliant and able to take care of yourself. In good weather it is wonderful scenery and challenging hiking, but in storms—that can occur even in summer—you must be able to protect yourself from the elements or escape to lower elevation.

---

61. **Greig Ridge:** Ted Greig of Royston was a hiker with a particular interest in the flowers of this ridge. The name is pronounced "Greg".

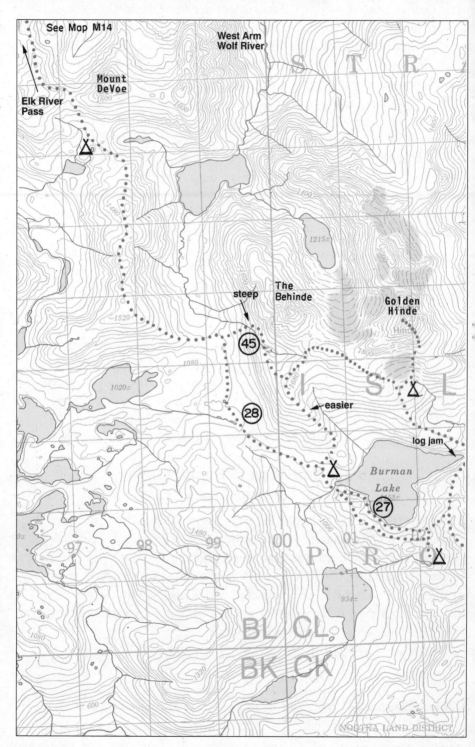

See Map M14

West Arm
Wolf River

Mount
DeVoe

Elk River
Pass

The
Behinde

steep

Golden
Hinde

45

1020±

28

easier

log jam

Burman
Lake

27

97   98   99   00   01

934±

BL CL
BK CK

NOOTKA LAND DISTRICT

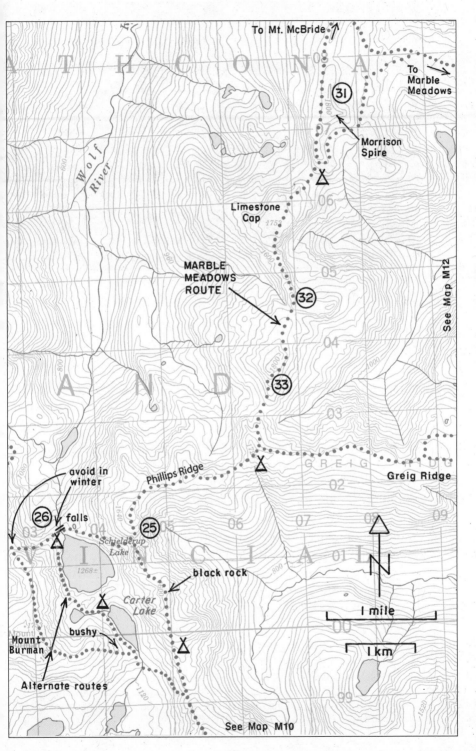

Golden Hinde from the south.   GIL PARKER

TRAIL From Arnica Lake, head north and contour west along Phillips Ridge. On map M10 on page 75, above the sizeable Harvey Lake, angle northwest and pass the route from Bedwell Lake that climbs up to the ridge north of the lake.

After about 1½ km, an alternate route to Schjelderup[62] Lake drops to the west, avoiding the route-finding difficulties and steep, treacherous terrain of the main route, as follows. From the lowest point on Phillips Ridge, map M13, [10U305206/5499314NAD83] [10U305200/5499100NAD27] descend the steep gully to the west for about 80 m and then traverse to the right at a descending angle towards a point below the outlet of Carter[63] Lake. Cross two branches of the stream, climb up to Carter Lake and contour around the southwest side of the lake in open terrain.

There is good camping at the lake's north end. Follow the stream up to another small lake under Mount Burman (summit is 1756 m) and then traverse a small ridge to Schjelderup Lake. Contour around the lake on the west side staying about 40-50 m above the lake for the easiest line to a camping area.㉖

---

62. **Schjelderup Lake:** In 1937, 16 year old Roger Schjelderup camped here with Sid Williams and Geoff Capes when they climbed the Golden Hinde. Later, in W.W. II, he rose to the rank of Colonel and was the most decorated Canadian officer.
63. **Carter Lake:** Frank Carter was killed in W.W. II.

A second alternate route swings west at the outlet of Carter Lake and climbs up and over Mount Burman to rejoin the main route to Burman Lake about a kilometre west of Schjelderup Lake. This second choice passes close to Mount Burman's summit of fine, granite boulders and many hikers prefer this traverse. It avoids the thrash around Schjelderup Lake and there is only one big hump to negotiate rather than three. The route is bushy near Carter Lake's south end. Both alternates avoid a significant elevation gain along Phillips Ridge going north and, more importantly, some very difficult route-finding between the col ㉕ at the north end of the ridge and Schjelderup Lake.

The traditional route follows Phillips Ridge northwards over a region of black rock to the col east of Schjelderup Lake.㉕ (The Marble Meadows route continues north from this point.) Proceeding toward the Golden Hinde[64] area, find a game trail leading steeply down through the meadows and follow it to the end of the meadows and through a thick grove of trees to a very steep grassy clearing with a stream on the right (north). Cross the stream. The route heads to the northwest under the last set of cliffs at about 1420 m to gain a side ridge coming up from the lake outlet. The trick is to go below the cliffs, otherwise you bluff out later, but do not drop down too far and miss the easier section through mature timber on a relatively obscure ridge. Follow down this, just north of centre. As with most east-west ridges between 1080 m and 1540 m in this area, there is clear going just north of ridge centre, due to heavy snow pack. The other side is often bushy.

Some travellers prefer to bypass the somewhat hair-raising drop from the Phillips Ridge to Schjelderup Lake. They start their descent about the 1600 m mark north of the black rock, south of point ㉕. From this point a long snow gully, partly scree in late summer, descends in a generally westerly direction to the bridge of land between Schjelderup and Carter lakes. Watch for an old CDMC sign on a tree near Schjelderup Lake's southwest corner. This route is not shown on map M13. These three descent routes are the most commonly used, but there are other variations, depending upon the skills of the party and the conditions encountered.

Follow the west shore of the lake to point ㉖. This route depends on the amount of residual snow there is, but even in summer there should be

---

64. **Golden Hinde:** Vancouver Island's highest peak was known to alpinists as "Rooster's Comb" until 1939, when it was officially named the Golden Hinde after the ship in which Sir Francis Drake circumnavigated the globe.

DESCENT POINT
TO CARTER LAKE

Phillips Ridge from Carter Lake.   MARTIN SMITH

only a couple of short, bushy sections. From the campsite at Schjelderup Lake's outlet go up the northeast ridge of Mount Burman, where there is clear going on the northwest side. Contour to the west under a steep section to a good ledge leading up and across to join the north ridge below cliffs at 1540 m. Follow this ridge down for about 100 m, then turn west down to meadows above the south bay of Burman Lake. An easy way down may be hard to find, as this is in a zone of glaciated granite.

If backpacking to the Golden Hinde (2200 m), continue down the north ridge to a log jam at the east end of Burman Lake. If you are bush-bashing, and dangling down steep bits holding on to saplings like a trout on a hook, you are probably on the route. Follow up the open ridge to the base of Golden Hinde, camping near a small lake on the south side of the mountain. The ascent of Golden Hinde is usually made via its southeast gully or ridge. To access this route climb directly above a small lake to the east and enter the northernmost gully on the southeast side.

13.c Burman Lake to Elk River Pass
Map M13 (also map M14)

DESCRIPTION This is a continuation of the routes from Bedwell Lake, from Myra Falls mine site, or from Marble Meadows all of which join at or near Burman Lake. This route goes from Burman Lake through to Elk River Pass, and from there down the Elk River to the Gold River Highway 28. The Elk River portion of this traverse is described in Sections 14 and 15. The Elk River is relatively accessible for day hikes or short backpacking trips, while the south part, as described in this section, is remote backcountry.

TRAIL From the campsite north of Burman Lake, contour northwest past the small lake directly southwest of The Behinde (1989 m) and follow the northeast side of the outflow stream.㊺ This is a very tricky spot. The route is exposed, and goes down and left, over the rocks before you reach the next stream. Two-thirds of the way down cut left into a shallow but reassuring crack, which returns you to the outflow stream. A rope can be very useful here. Descend the huge snow, or boulder, bowl to rejoin the direct route from Burman Lake. An easier descent, if longer, follows a descending ridge southeast to the outlet at the west end of Burman Lake, where there are camping options.

From the meadow above the south bay of Burman Lake, en route from Schjelderup Lake, contour west at the 1230 m level and follow the northwest ridge of Mount Burman to the outlet of Burman Lake. This is not as even as it appears on the map, due to granite bluffs. Alternately, work down to the southwest bay ㉗ and follow the shoreline to the outlet.

From the west end of Burman Lake hike north, up through open areas to about the 1230 m level. Drop down a little, turn west and, at the 1200 m level, contour below the rock bluffs. Game trails and old tapes make the route fairly easy to follow where gullies must be crossed. At the heather meadows west of the Golden Hinde, turn north at the first small lake, keeping to an open area below some rock slides.㉘ A fairly level route at the 1200 m level leads to a big rockslide coming off the west side of The Behinde peak.

Cross at the base of this slide and up to a saddle between Burman (west) and Wolf River (north) watersheds. Hike west across this and up the southeast ridge of an unnamed mountain at the head of the Ucona River. Keep to the centre of this ridge, but go to the right at one steep spot at the 1350 m level. Near the south summit, turn north. Traverse the many small summits and descend a connecting ridge to Mount DeVoe (1710 m). At the lowest point, go northwest, to contour around the meadows above some small lakes at 1260 m, where you can make a good camp, then north, following a creek not shown on NTS maps, up to a small col on the west ridge of Mount DeVoe. Turn sharply west up a steep heather slope to about the 1600 m level, then turn north and follow the ridge centre.

When you are overlooking a large round lake at the head of the west fork of Wolf River, (on map M14, page 100) hike northwest down a side ridge to the southwest corner of this lake.㉙ This is a good camping area. The route then follows the west side of this lake across an overgrown slide area at the base of a prominent cliff, and up through a strip of timber on the west side of a small creek. Staying in the creek bed itself is a preferred option. At the top, a good game trail continues along the west side of a small lake, then northwest across flower meadows and, keeping right and in the trees, up a final 220 m to Elk River Pass.

NOTES For those going south from the Elk River Pass, your best route drops steeply down the heather before angling left, through mature forest, towards Golden Hinde, which you can now see in the far distance. You should stay well above and to the left of a prominent rock cliff directly below. It is easier to cross creeks and stay in the forest, rather than getting into a creek gully and following it down.

Aerial view of Della Falls, Della Lake and Nine Peaks.   GIL PARKER

14

Elk River
(Landslide Lake)

The Elk River Pass is a spectacular place, with a view to the south of all the peaks you have passed, the most prominent being the Golden Hinde. To the east is the double summit of Rambler Peak, and ahead, down the valley, Elkhorn is on the right (east) and the rugged face of Mount Colonel Foster is on the left (west).

14.a Upper Elk River   Map M14

DESCRIPTION The Elk River Valley is a popular area for day hiking, for short backpacking trips, and for access to the high mountains on either side of the valley. Though part of a main route to the Golden Hinde, about three days one way, the Elk River Trail is used mostly by those who want to hike in to Landslide Lake or access the mountains on either side of the valley. Hikers can camp en route and take a daypack on the second day, either camping a second night or heading out.

BC Parks has established a fee collection zone and a no-camping area for the Elk River corridor. Use only the designated campsites at Butterwort Creek (map M14) and the Upper Gravel Bar, below Landslide Lake. Camping is not allowed at Landslide Lake or at the glacial lake at the foot of Mount Colonel Foster. The camping fee in the Elk River corridor is $5 per person over age 15, per night (2008).

TRAIL Descending the pass, be cautious of crossing old spring snow which has been undercut by the river. After the upper canyon, the route follows the east side of the river, sometimes high up the side. Tape markers can usually be seen. Cross to the west side of the river to avoid steep cliffs, then recross to the east side and continue down to several

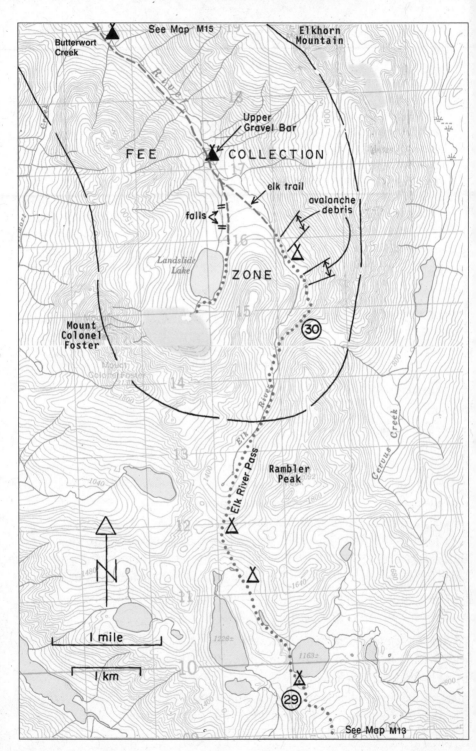

Butterwort Creek

See Map M15

Elkhorn Mountain

Upper Gravel Bar

FEE   COLLECTION

elk trail

avalanche debris

falls

Landslide Lake

ZONE

30

Mount Colonel Foster

Mount Colonel Foster

Elk River Pass

Rambler Peak

Cervus Creek

N

1 mile

1 km

29

See Map M13

recent avalanche debris zones.㉚ A bypass route leads through one of the larger ones to a campsite. There are two more slide zones and rock slides to negotiate, so be alert and watch for new bypass routes. Eventually you will find an elk trail which enters the forest about 100 m up on the west bank of the Elk River. You can follow this down through the forest to the junction of the stream from Landslide Lake. The main valley trail begins here across the BC Parks bridge and follows the west bank of the Elk River.

> NOTE On the east side of the outfall stream from Landslide Lake, a trail climbs to the side of a waterfall, very impressive in flood, and leads to the lake. Camping at Landslide Lake is not permitted but it is a spectacular place to visit. For those en route to, or from, the Golden Hinde this makes a pleasant lunch break provided backpacks are stashed and not carried up to the lake and then down again.

Landslide Lake below Mount Colonel Foster. LINDSAY ELMS

15

Lower Elk River

15.a Lower Elk River   Map M15

DESCRIPTION This is a lovely valley and many hikers travel it every summer. Providing access to the spectacular peaks on either side of the valley, and an excellent backpacking experience for those who choose to hike, the Elk River valley is one of the best access points for entry into the western part of Strathcona Park. (See also Section 14.)

During the strong earthquake of June 24, 1946, a part of Mount Colonel Foster[65] (2135 m) fell away into Landslide Lake below. The water was displaced so violently that it caused havoc in this part of the valley, taking out hundreds of trees, down to bedrock, for about 800 m. This scar is still clearly visible; see photograph, page 101.

BC Parks has established a fee collection zone and a no-camping area for the Elk River corridor. Due to the popularity of this trail, BC Parks has developed management strategies to protect the area from the effects of human use and abuse. Use only the designated campsites at Butterwort Creek and the Upper Gravel Bar, below Landslide Lake. Camping is not allowed at Landslide Lake or at the glacial lake at the foot of Mount Colonel Foster. The camping fee in the Elk River Trail corridor is $5 per person over age 15, per night.

ACCESS From the Buttle Narrows bridge, 47.7 km west of the Campbell River junction of Highways 19 and 28, stay on Highway 28 and continue another 23.7 km west toward Gold River. Watch for signs to the trailhead.

---

65. **Colonel William W. Foster** (later Major-General) (1875-1954) served as BC Deputy Minister of Public Works, as a distinguished soldier in W.W. I, as Vancouver Police Chief, but it was as Billy Foster that he participated in first ascents of Mount Robson and Mount Logan. He was president of the ACC 1922-1924.

Driving time from Campbell River is about 1 hour. The trailhead is 16 km east of Gold River.

TRAIL The trail is essentially an old elk trail that has been improved over the years, first by a government crew, then by some members of the Island Mountain Ramblers (IMR), the CDMC, and by BC Parks. The trail is seasonally cleared up to the gravel bar below Landslide Lake and upper river flats. It is now quite a good trail and the hazardous log crossings at Butterwort[66], Volcano and Puzzle creeks have been replaced by sturdy bridges built by the IMR in conjunction with BC Parks. At Volcano Creek there have been numerous bear sightings. The lake looks just like a volcano.

It is about a three-hour hike for a hiker with full overnight gear to the Butterwort Creek gravel bar, or about six hours to the Upper Gravel Bar Campsite. From here you can make day excursions, especially to Landslide Lake. Also from here, the route up the Elk River Valley and south to the Golden Hinde continues up to Elk River Pass. (See Section 14.a.)

15.b Kings[67] Peak Map M15

DESCRIPTION This trail is steep in sections and most groups with full pack will take 5 to 6 hours to reach the upper bowl. In the spring, caution is required where the trail opens into a curved gully just below the north bowl. Avalanches can funnel into the gully, from which hikers have no fast exit.

ACCESS On Highway 28, drive approximately 19.5 km west from the Buttle Narrows bridge and turn left on the Elk River Timber (ERT) logging road (just after the highway passes under a power transmission line). One kilometre later, park at a pull-off on the left before the logging road crosses the Elk River.

TRAIL/ROUTE Just beyond the power line clearing, the trail climbs to a small creek crossing and joins the access route on the other side. An alternative is to drive the power line dirt road, where the gate may be locked, and link up with the standard route as shown on the map.

---

66. **Common butterwort** (*Pinguicula vulgaris*) grows along the banks of the creek. It is an insect-eating plant with single purple flowers on stems above fleshy leaves. (ref. Plants of Coastal British Columbia by Pojar and MacKinnon.)
67. **Kings Peak:** Michael and James King were on the Ellison expedition in the region in 1910.

After reaching the snow bowl, near the campsite in the meadow, it is safer to take the West Ridge summer route rather than continuing south up the gully route. During the winter or even late spring, the gully is dangerous and prone to avalanches.

The summer route crosses the north bowl in a southwest direction. Go up a small hill and through a band of trees (remnant flags) to access a large hanging valley directly north of the feature known locally as "The Queen" or "The Queen's Ridge." From here cross the drainage and climb a distinct route to the valley's southwest corner. Ascend an obvious, long, straight gully to the top of the ridge. A good "bivvy boulder" (place to bivouac, or shelter, during bad weather or emergency) sits beside the trail on the flat bench about halfway between the crest of the gully and "The Queen." The route winds around the back (southwest) side of the ridge, then goes almost directly over the summit of "The Queen", and drops into the col between "The Queen" and Kings Peak, then up to the top of Kings Peak (2065 m).

In the winter, avalanches threaten the gully and lower approaches. The West Ridge Winter Route begins farther down the valley, enters a short gully and continues up to the ridge. There are no ribbons and the start of the trail is hard to find. This route has been adopted by The Heathens Mountaineering Club[68].

15.c Elkhorn Mountain   Map M15

DESCRIPTION   The route to the summit of Elkhorn Mountain (2166 m) is mainly for climbers. From the campsite it is 4 to 5 hours to the summit. There is lots of exposure, loose rock, possible rappels and intricate route finding—serious stuff. Caution is required, and the assurance of a climbing rope. The climb of Elkhorn[69] Mountain is not a hike. However, the route to the lower part of the mountain and to some decent camping with great views is a reasonable hiking objective.

TRAIL   Follow the Elk River Trail for 2½ km and cross the river to where the route begins on the south side of a prominent creek. This route to the

---

68. **Heathens Club:** The club's name refers to those who prefer "the heath", or the high places where heather grows, not necessarily to the philosophical beliefs of the members.

69. **Elkhorn Mountain:** Named by members of the ACC 1912 first ascent party. Known as "the Matterhorn of the Park," and close to the Elk River, the name "Elkhorn" was chosen.

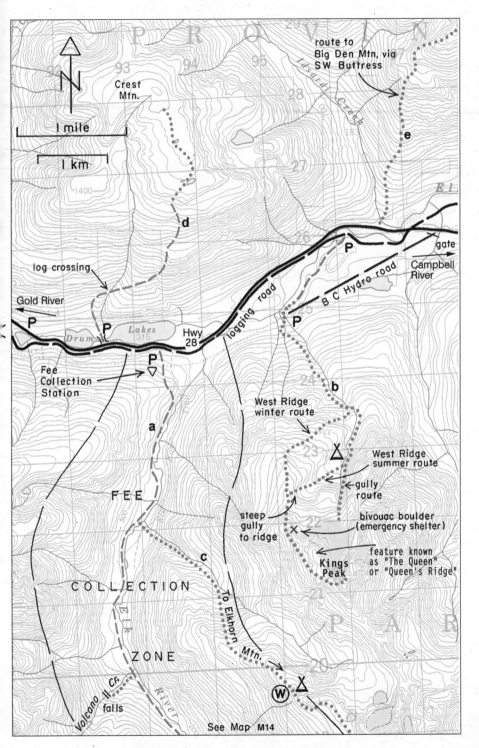

northwest ridge is fairly obvious and flagged in places. Stay to the right at steep sections. Most groups with full packs will take six to seven hours to reach the usual campsite (see map M15). On a clear day you will be able to see Elkhorn Mountain (Vancouver Island's second highest peak), Kings Peak, Mount Colonel Foster and possibly Victoria Peak.

15.d Crest Mountain   Map M15

TRAIL From the Buttle Narrows bridge, stay on Highway 28 and drive just under 25 km to the Drum Lake Narrows. Watch for the signposted parking area. Cross the Narrows by bridge north onto a clearly defined trail that is graded at the lower levels. The trail was originally constructed by the BC Forest Service for a study of climatic conditions. No longer used for this purpose, the trail has deteriorated higher up. About a kilometre in, a tree has been felled to cross the creek, but it is not always needed. Beyond this level the trail becomes steep, but even those who do not go up the whole way will find there are some fine viewpoints.

Time up to 1440 m level and an alpine lake is about four hours. If you continue another kilometre you will reach the rounded top. On good days there are spectacular views in all directions, especially south across the valley towards Kings Peak, Elkhorn Mountain and Mount Colonel Foster.

NOTE Crest Creek Crags, 2.5 km west of the Crest Mountain Trail, has become a very well known rock climbing area, mainly developed by The Heathens, a climbing club from Campbell River. However, non-designated camping within one kilometre of a highway is not allowed in BC's provincial parks, so you are advised not to camp here. BC Parks closely monitors this area.

15.e Big Den Mountain   Map M15

This is another route to the north of Highway 28 on a south-facing slope with great views into the Park across the Highway. On Highway 28, drive 20 km west of the Buttle Narrows bridge (500 m past the turn off for Kings Peak access on the Elk River Timber road). The route leaves the Highway climbing north on the east side of Idsardi Creek. Follow the southwest buttress north to the 1520 m level, then angle right generally northeast to open terrain and a plateau summit.

15.f Lady Falls   (Not shown on our maps)

On Highway 28, drive 16.7 km west of the Buttle Narrows bridge. Watch for the parking area, on the left side of the highway. A short but steep trail climbs up to Lady Falls, a clamorous cascade on Cervus[70] Creek. Stay well back from the cliff.

15.g Donner Lake   (Not shown on our maps)

DESCRIPTION Donner Lake is a popular fishing destination and a canoe/hiking access route into Strathcona Park mountains. The lake is accessed by old logging roads, which are in poor condition, sometimes washed out and impassable by vehicle. The area reached by the road seems to be used by the four wheel drive party crowd, and you should be cautious about leaving your vehicle, or camping overnight. Locked gates may restrict access.

ACCESS In the town of Gold River, heading west, take the second left turn after the arena entrance, onto a paved road (Ucona Main) signed "To the Recycling Plant". Stay on this road (now dirt) for 12 km to Star Lake. Three kilometres past the lake, take the first left turn (U7 off Ucona Main). From here, a high-slung four wheel drive vehicle is needed. Next, turn right onto the Western Forest Products (WFP) road to Kunlin Lake and drive around the lake to Donner Falls. Park here and walk up beside the river to Donner Lake.

---

70. **Cervus** is Latin for "deer" and the local elk are *Cervus Canadensis*.

16

Gold River Area

Gold River is the end of Highway 28 from Campbell River and is located at the head of Muchalat Inlet with ferry access to Nootka Island and Tahsis. To the south of Gold River there is access to Mounts Donner and Matchlee; to the north Gold Lake and Victoria Peak. At one time the only road route to the north Island ran north from Gold River, but now that Highway 19 connects to Port McNeill and Port Hardy, most traffic goes that way. However, the Nimpkish Road provides access north to Woss and Tahsis and many interesting mountain regions.

The Tahsis Lions Club's annual "Great Walk" follows the Head Bay FSR for 63.5 km, all the way from Gold River to Tahsis. To learn more about this fund-raising trek, touted as North America's toughest pledge walk, contact the Tahsis Lions Club, PO Box 430, Tahsis, BC V0P 1X0.

16.a Gold Lake   Map M16A

DESCRIPTION Visited mainly by anglers, the region has stands of old-growth trees and is home to Roosevelt elk. There are two routes into Gold Lake[71]. Due to limited trail clearing and maintenance both accesses are overgrown and hard to locate. Snowfall in this area is abundant and the snowpack holds into late June. Expect rougher roads closer to Gold Lake. A high four wheel drive vehicle may be required.

ACCESS FROM THE EAST From the junction of Highway 19 and Highway 28 in Campbell River, drive north on Highway 19 for about 14.5 km to the Island Timberlands Menzies (Salmon River) Main. Check on access and road conditions with Island Timberlands (North) if your hike is planned early in the year. Use Island Timberlands Recreation and Logging Road Guide to TFL 39. (See Timber Companies on page 215.)

---

71. **Gold Lake** is named for the ore found here.

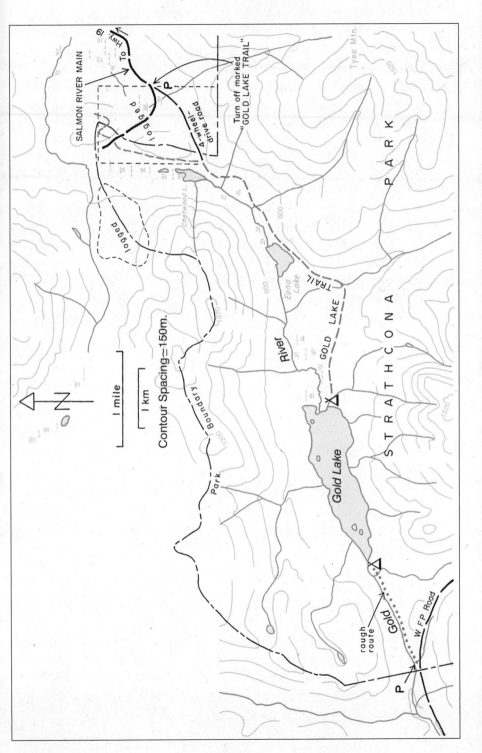

Turn left (west) onto Menzies (Salmon River) Main, past a company work yard and drive 15.2 km to Brewster Lake's south end. Cross the bridge and continue west another 30 km via the Salmon River and Grilse Creek valleys to the start of the trail signposted "Gold Lake Trail" at Spur H. There is limited parking here. Only four wheel drive vehicles can proceed along the nearby spur road. The Park boundary is about 2 km along this road, and the trail to the lake is about 6 km from here. There are camping options at the lake.

ACCESS FROM THE WEST Western Forest Products has opened access to the west side of Gold Lake with the construction of a logging road, which passes through the northwest corner of Strathcona Park to access timber outside the park boundary. The upper stretches may require a four wheel drive vehicle with good clearance. Use WFP's Visitors Guide to Logging Roads and Recreation Areas (Nootka Region), or other Map Sources listed in the Appendix, page 212.

Drive 3 km north from Gold River and cross the lofty Gold River bridge to a signposted T-junction. Swing right onto Nimpkish Road heading toward Woss. (A left goes to the Upana Caves and Tahsis.) About 6.5 km north from the Gold River bridge, cut right (east) onto East Main to begin the climb up the Gold River Valley. Keep right at the Y junction. The road cuts through Gold/Muchalat Provincial Park (653 ha). East Main has a strange one-way section that could be dangerous if you miss it and go the wrong way. A little before the Saunders Main junction you will cross Saunders Creek. At the junction, stay on East Main and travel approximately 2 km to the trailhead.

TRAIL The parking area is on the left side of the road. The trail is difficult to find and overgrown with bush. The route is in poor condition but the distance to Gold Lake is only 2 to 3 km. It is possible to camp at the lake.

16.b White Ridge Provincial Park (no map)

White Ridge Provincial Park (1343 ha), named for its white limestone and caves (part of the karst topography that exists here), is located between Strathcona Provincial Park's northwest boundary and Highway 28. It is located 4 km east of Gold River and is accessed off Gold River Highway 28 via the HBR 800 logging road.

This forested ridge is prime elk and deer habitat. There are no facilities or services and the area is not regularly patrolled.

Paul Erickson in meadows below Victoria Peak.   GIL PARKER

16.c Victoria Peak   Map M16C

DESCRIPTION Victoria Peak is a mountaineering objective southwest of Sayward or north of Gold River. However, the south ridge of Victoria Peak is a beautiful alpine ridge hike, with some easy scrambling up intermittent rock steps. The trailhead is at 1170 m and there is a good campsite at 1550 m next to some tarns on a semi-plateau. The hike is the easiest access to Victoria Peak, with a climbers' trail well flagged.

ACCESS From Gold River drive north, cross the Gold River bridge to a signposted T-junction where the road swings 180 degrees left. (A left turn goes to the Upana Caves and Tahsis.) Swing right onto Nimpkish Road heading toward Woss. Drive 6.5 km, making sure to take the Tsaxana bypass, then turn right on East Road. (Since July 2007, it is necessary to take East Road because it bypasses a washout on West Road.) After a further 13.6 km, turn left onto Waring Mainline. Drive 0.5 km, then turn right onto West Road. After 7.5 km, turn right onto W-79 at the end of West Road.

The road is driveable by a two wheel drive vehicle to here only, with active logging in the area. About 5.8 km up W-79 there is a washout, but it is negotiable by driving into the uphill side bush. The trailhead, at 1170 m, is only 1.4 km beyond that point.

TRAIL From the trailhead, hike almost due east and pick your way up through a steep area of logging slash to get onto the south ridge of Victoria Peak. Hike a short distance north to pick up an indistinct east-west ridge (remnant flags) and follow this 1 km east to the main divide, 3 km south of Victoria Peak. It should take about 30-45 minutes to gain the ridge. The trail through the heather is distinct. From here, the trail follows the south ridge, which gets quite narrow at times. There is good camping with space for two tents at a large tarn, which is located about two hours from the parking area.

Climbers planning to climb Victoria Peak often use this campsite. From here you can walk along the ridge for another one or two hours before you reach the massif itself and are faced with technical climbing. Many people day-hike to the south ridge, climb up close to Victoria Peak and then head back down. Allow four to five hours for a return hike.

NOTES Contact Western Forest Products in Gold River for updates on road conditions and access restrictions. (See Timber Companies in Appendix.)

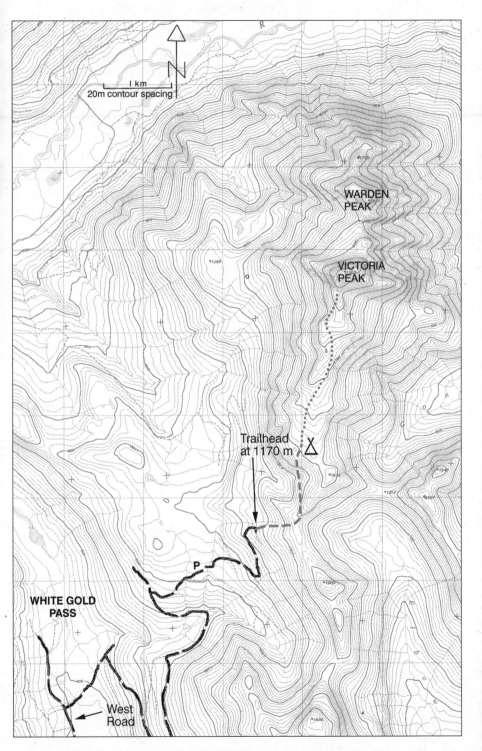

WARDEN PEAK

VICTORIA PEAK

Trailhead
at 1170 m

WHITE GOLD
PASS

West
Road

1 km
20m contour spacing

16.d Upana Caves   Map 16D

DESCRIPTION The Upana Caves are comprised of several individual caves ranging in size from single rooms to branching passages of varying length. There are 15 known entrances within the system, and the combined length of cave passages is approximately 450 m. Once at Upana Caves you have the opportunity to observe and explore a natural cave system. Pick up a self-guided tour brochure from the BCFS Campbell River District office or at a travel infocentre.

ACCESS The Upana Caves are located 17 km northwest of Gold River on the Head Bay Forest Road to Tahsis. Driving time from Gold River is 25 minutes. The trail is mostly a surface trail of about 400 m through an immature forest (replanted) setting.

CAUTION The first systematic exploration and mapping of these caves was undertaken in 1975 by recreational cavers. Spelunkers named the cave system after the Upana River, which flows through one of the caves. The cave interiors remain in a relatively wild, undeveloped state. It is very important that visitors be careful not to disturb the cave environment. Keep to the established trails and underground routes, do not touch delicate cave formations, and refrain from smoking and lighting fires.

To safely explore the caves you should carry a reliable flashlight or headlamp and at least two backup lights, which will help you to see the cave features and to watch your footing on uneven floors. The Upana Caves are a year-round experience. No matter what the weather is outside, the temperature inside the caves averages a chilly 7° Celsius, so bring a sweater or jacket.

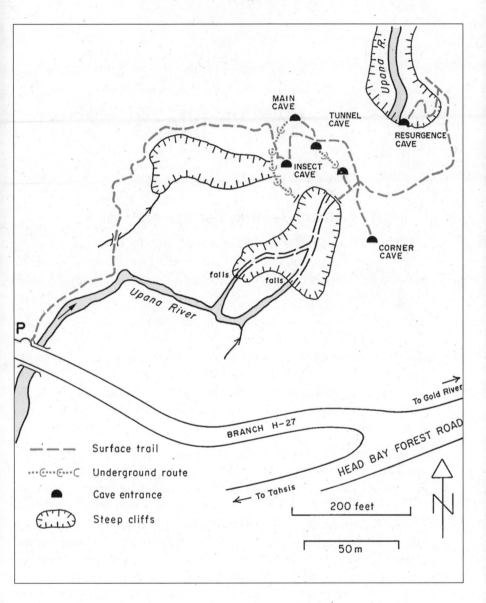

MAIN CAVE
TUNNEL CAVE
RESURGENCE CAVE
INSECT CAVE
CORNER CAVE
Upana R.
falls
falls
Upana River
P

To Gold River
BRANCH H-27
HEAD BAY FOREST ROAD
To Tahsis

Surface trail
Underground route
Cave entrance
Steep cliffs

200 feet
50 m

N

17

Hornby Island

17.a Mount Geoffrey Escarpment Map M17

DESCRIPTION On Hornby Island myriad trails for horses, bicycles and hikers cover the Mount Geoffrey Escarpment Provincial Park and the adjacent Regional Park, with Georgia Strait views from the south ridge hikers' trails.

ACCESS Hornby Island is reached by the Denman Island ferry, and a drive across Denman to the Hornby Island ferry. From the ferry landing drive left (north) on Shingle Spit Road to Central Road, and turn right to four entry points at Lea Smith Road, at Joe King Park, at Slade Road and at Strachan Road. Secure the map of Hornby, sold locally, to decipher the complex of trails, or a map and pamphlet from the Regional District of Comox Strathcona.

TRAILS From the ferry landing turn immediately right to the Shingle Spit Trail, a 2.3 km trail to Ford Cove which connects to Central Road. If you turn left, then immediately right onto Mount Road, you will reach the start of the Bench Trail, a 3 km easy trail exiting at Evston or Strachan Road. The most challenging, sometimes precipitous, trail begins at Lea Smith Road. The technical 3.2 km Cliff Trail follows the west boundary of the park, reaching a parking area near Mount Road. Connect from here to the moderate Ridge Trail, about 2.6 km, along the top of the southwest ridge. The multi-use Summit Trail parallels the Ridge Trail, often in timber, but with scenic openings above Ridge Trail.

17.b Helliwell Park (not on our maps)

On the east end of Hornby Island a gently-graded easy trail follows the coast line in a 3 km loop along the south and east shores of the Island. Access is from the end of Helliwell, off Anderson, which in turn is off St. Johns Point Road.

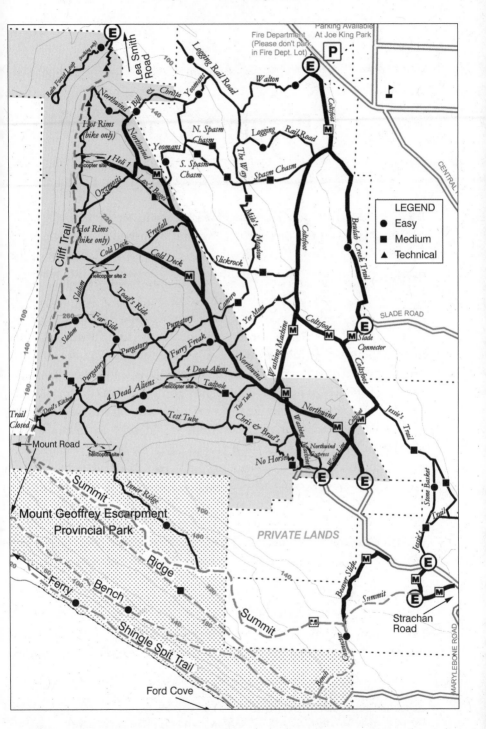

18

Beaufort Range

DESCRIPTION Extending from Horne[72] Lake in the south to Cumberland in the north, the Beaufort[73] Range has been well used by climbers and hikers. Over the years several hiking clubs have cleared some of the overgrown logging roads and built trails to some of the most beautiful places on the range.

ACCESS East side access is from near Fanny Bay and the Rosewall Creek area via the Horne/Bowser Forest Service Road. Mount Joan, (1557 m) highest mountain in the Beaufort Range, and Mount Curran (1478 m), have established trails. Further to the north, trails have been created on Mount Clifton (1420 m) and Mount Chief Frank (1470 m).

West side access is from the Beaver Creek road and the Comox Main (Island Timberlands). Drive 4.2 km from the "Y fork" coming into Port Alberni on Highway 4, cross the Kitsuksis Creek bridge and take the next right onto Beaver Creek Road. About 16.5 km on this road, turn right on the gravel Somers Road. This is Kilometre Zero on Comox Main, from which point distances are measured. (CX108 is Comox Main 10.8 km.) Branch roads off Comox Main generally need four wheel drive vehicles.

Rosewall Creek Provincial Park (54 ha), close to the Highway 19 turn-off, features a picturesque 2 km trail along Rosewall Creek to a waterfall. There is a wheelchair path.

Horne Lake Caves Provincial Park is located 60 km north of Nanaimo and 26 km west of Qualicum. The park can be accessed via the Horne Lake exit off Hwy 19 or Hwy 19A. Follow signs for 12 km to Horne Lake. There are 1.3 km of hiking trails. Also there is world-class spelunking,

---

72. **Adam Horne** (1831-1903) discovered the lake in 1856.
73. **Sir Francis Beaufort** (1774-1857) was a hydrographer with the Royal Navy.

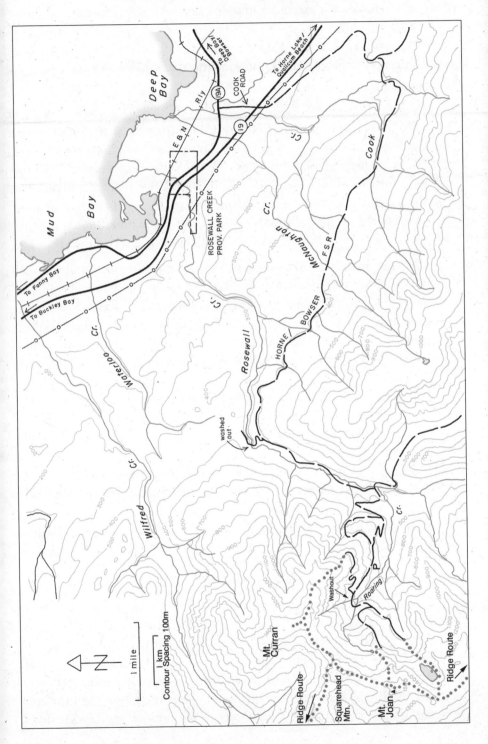

self-guided or via extensive tours by contacting the operator at (250) 248-7829.

Near Horne Lake is a Regional Park (105.3 ha.) For more information contact the Regional District of Nanaimo at (250) 752-7199.

18.a Mount Joan   Map M18A

ACCESS From the Island Highway 19, turn west at the lights at the Cook Road intersection, near Fanny Bay. At the T-junction turn left onto the gravel logging road and follow it 2 km to the next junction. Take the right fork down the bank. From the highway drive 14.8 km and take the right fork just before the bridge that crosses Rosewall Creek. The road switchbacks up the ridge north of Roaring Creek, to a limited parking area on a major right turn, where the trail leads off left (westward).

TRAILS Signs in an alder clearing indicate the trail junction for Mount Joan and Mount Curran. For Mount Joan follow the sign and trail (old road) to a major washout at Roaring Creek. The trail descends to the creek then up a steep bank on the other side. Continue up the logging road as it switchbacks higher. The trail veers off up the bank to the right through a clearcut and into the old-growth trees on the left-hand side.

The trail steepens to a little saddle overlooking small tarns in a basin below Mount Joan and Squarehead Mountain. From the tarns follow the small creek into the upper meadows and up a spur onto the ridge just to the north of Mount Joan. On the summit, an easy ridge walk, is a radio repeater tower.

An easy 1.2 km ridge walk to the north leads to the summit of Squarehead Mountain. Mount Curran is accessible from Squarehead Mountain and requires climbing down into the intervening saddle and then up a steep ridge, which leads to some small tarns on Mount Curran's summit ridge.

18.b Mount Curran   Map M18A

From the Mount Joan/Mount Curran junction in the alder clearing (see Mount Joan Trail description, preceding section) veer right up the logging road and follow several switchbacks to the end of the road. On the left the trail climbs through some second-growth timber into a small patch of old-growth and into an old burned area on the southeast ridge. Eventually the trail exits the burn and enters the forest, then the sub-alpine area. The trail becomes harder to see but look for flagging in the trees and rock cairns higher up. Once in the alpine follow the ridge to the northwest past several inviting tarns to a wide-open summit.

18.c Mount Clifton   Map M18B

ACCESS To access from the **east** start at the traffic lights on Island Highway 19 at the Buckley Bay/Denman Island ferry intersection and turn inland up Buckley Bay Main. There is a manned gate on the logging road in an area where TimberWest is logging. Access might vary from weekends only, to no access. (Call ahead, see page 215, for logging companies.)

Continue along Buckley Bay Main past Sheila Lake Main to the sign that says "Lunchtime Lake" to the left. The road heads around the north side of the lake. A high-slung four wheel drive vehicle is required beyond Lunchtime Lake. About half a kilometre beyond the lake a road to the left crosses the creek and starts winding up towards Kim Lake, which is tucked in behind a small hill. At the end of the road, about 1 km, pick up the flagged trail to Kim Lake.

TRAIL The trail heads around the north side of Kim Lake and then climbs a steep, northeast-sloping spur. Once in the alpine the summit is about 400 m to the west. There is a well-built cairn on the summit and a register.

ACCESS To access from the **west**, drive north on Comox Main, and turn right on CX165 (old branch 132 which should join branch 116). Follow this logging road, gaining elevation, generally up the southeast side of Katlum Creek. The road begins to descend into a broad valley between Clifton and Chief Frank. Park at a washout.

TRAIL Hike up the road about 30 minutes, into the forest up to a saddle, then right, through sub alpine vegetation and onto a wooded slope of Mount Clifton. There are views from the summit northwest to Strathcona Park, and east to the coast. The several tarns below on the west are called Three Heathers Lake.

18.d Mount Chief Frank   Map M18B

ACCESS See east access for Mount Clifton, preceding section. Inquire of TimberWest about access through their manned gate. The route to the trail for Mount Chief Frank also turns off the Island Highway at the intersection at Buckley Bay and follows Buckley Bay Main. At the 16 km

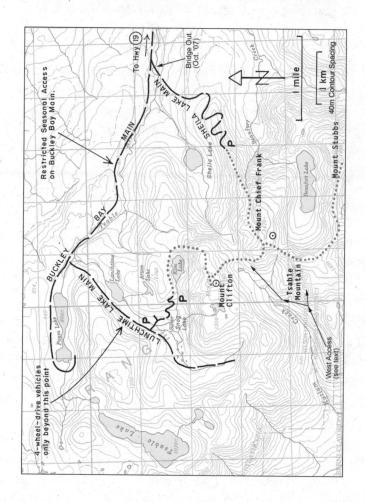

mark turn left onto Sheila Lake Main and cross the Tsable River. At last report the bridge was out here, so it may be a long hike. It is about 4 km on the old road to the trailhead. On the logging road, take the second left and follow small rock cairns that have been placed on the side of the road at each corner to indicate which road to take.

TRAILS The trail from the east side begins high on the ridge at a turnaround at the end of the road. Initially the trail is not well defined as it climbs through big old-growth timber but watch for flagging tape on the trees. At 1100 m the trail becomes obvious as it climbs through a narrow section of the ridge and up a short, steep little bluff. Above this the trail continues up to the base of the bluffs at 1240 m.

Tsable and Chief Frank mountains above Beaufort Lake.   RANDY CHURCH

There are two routes up to the summit. The first and most frequently used route angles up the benches under the north face and around to the northwest side of the mountain. Ascend through easy heather benches onto the summit ridge and angle east for 500 m to the summit. A large rock cairn, with a register, is on the summit.

The second route cuts out to the left at the base of the bluffs. Drop down into the head of a small creek and climb up the other side. Continue working your way under the bluffs to another small creek. Cross this stream then get out onto a small spur that leads onto heather slopes and then angles up to the summit. This route is not flagged but makes for an interesting traverse of the mountain.

From the west approach to Clifton (Section 18.c) one can climb from the parking spot at the washout to the right directly up steep clearcut, then forest onto a wooded ridge running to Tsable Mountain. This is an access to the traverse described in the next section, from Tsable to Stubbs and eventually to Mount Apps and the southern part of the Beaufort Range.

18.e Mount Clifton to Mount Joan
(part shown on maps)

ROUTE DESCRIPTION Although this traverse is rarely hiked and is not well flagged, it is a beautiful high-level traverse of the Beaufort Range. Beginning at the trailhead for Mount Clifton follow the trail past Kim Lake and up to the summit of the mountain. Descend the south side to a saddle at the head of Katlum Creek and then up onto Mount Chief Frank. It is not necessary to go to this summit as the route descends through steep bluffs to the southwest to a saddle between Mount Chief Frank and Tsable Mountain. It is an easy climb up to the summit of Tsable Mountain where there is a repeater tower. Look for carvings on some of the trees with the names and dates of the surveyors from the 1940s.

From the top of Tsable Mountain the route continues to the south along a wide spur over to Mount Stubbs. There are no campsites along this route but there are numerous small tarns that are idyllic to camp beside.

From the top of Mount Stubbs descend south of the mountain and follow the ridge towards Mount Henry Spencer. This is not flagged. From Mount Henry Spencer follow the ridge to the southeast going up and down numerous small mountains until Mount Apps is reached at the head of Tumblewater Creek. (See west access, below.) Descend south of the summit onto a wide meadow with lots of little tarns and ponds. This is another beautiful place to camp.

Continue south out of the meadows and into the forest, then down to a saddle at the head of Wilfred Creek (1190 m). Now begins the climb up the northwest spur to the summit of Squarehead Mountain. From Squarehead Mountain climb over to Mount Joan and from the trail there, down to the east side logging roads and trailhead.

ACCESS FROM WEST In addition to the north and south ends, there is an access from the west side to Mount Apps, towards the middle of this traverse. From the kilometre zero on Comox Main (end of the paved Beaver Creek Road) drive north to CX91 (old branch 113), turn right and continue 2.5 km until stopped by an old washout at 10.5 km.

TRAIL Hike the low (right) road for about 30 minutes to a wood sign "Trail." Climb left into a clearcut, then a forest to a ridge. After a kilometre or two the trail reaches the subalpine. Just before a tarn, flagging directs you left to a higher bench and Lake Zella. Follow around the right side, then up a ridge running north to a major peak, then down, and up again to the large cairn on Mount Apps.

19

Seal Bay
Regional Park

19. Seal Bay Regional Park
(Xwee Xwhwa Luq)   Map M19

DESCRIPTION Xwee Xwhwa Luq is a Salish name suggested by the Comox Band meaning, "place with an atmosphere of peace and serenity." Seal Bay Regional Park is administered as a nature park by the Regional District of Comox-Strathcona. Of its 714 ha, the Crown Land portion (564 ha) is managed under a Licence of Occupation. Situated near Seal Bay, just 15 minutes north of Courtenay or Comox, the original trails were constructed between 1971 and 1973 by the Comox Valley Naturalists Society. Seasonal trail maintenance is done mainly by volunteers.

Newcomers are recommended to access the park at the main parking area, on Bates Road, coming in via Anderton or Coleman roads. Other access points are Clark, Elmo, Fitzell, Hardy, Huband, Loxley, Seabank and Seacliff roads.

TRAILS The park has 25 km of trails, including some bike/horse trails on the perimeter. Yellow markers indicate these multi-use trails. The core area is for hikers only. No camping, hunting, fires or motorized vehicles are allowed. Remember to leash all dogs. The park is closed from 11 pm to 6:30 am. Be cautious near the ravines and keep well back from undercut banks.

Map M19 Seal Bay Regional Park

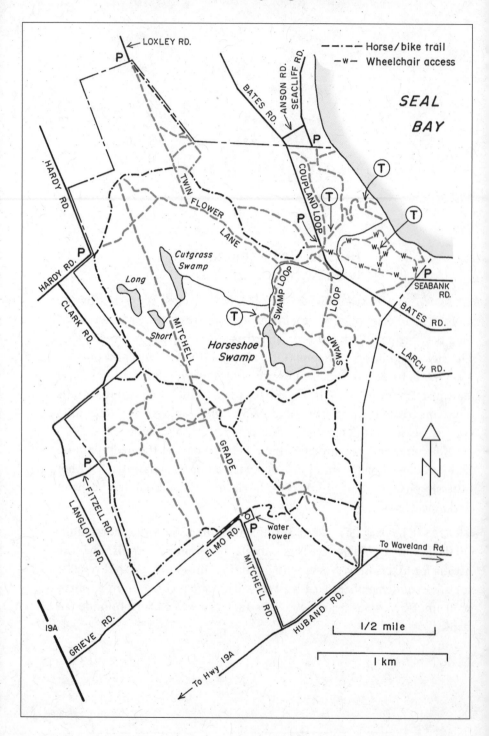

20

Quadra Island

See Regional Map M21, page 141

Just over two hundred years ago, Captain Vancouver made contact with the aboriginal people. He sent yawls (a type of small boat) through Discovery Passage from the north before he brought in his ship, "Discovery", and anchored off Cape Mudge[74], the south tip of the island. Today the village of We-Wai-kai offers visitors a modern museum displaying outstanding examples of aboriginal art, returned from Ottawa where they had been held since being confiscated by the RCMP in 1921.

DESCRIPTION Quadra Island[75] is a short ferry ride across Discovery Passage from Campbell River. The island offers many recreational opportunities including coastal kayaking, diving, fishing, lake boating and hiking. The trails and routes described are measured from Heriot Bay store, near the ferry to Cortez Island. All the trails are well signed. Routes, which may not be maintained or signed, are usually only suitable for experienced hikers.

Volunteers maintain official "gazetted" trails, particularly onerous after serious windstorms cause blowdowns. The descriptions given here might be affected by expanded logging operations.

Generally these trails and routes are located on Crown land, which is managed by the Ministry of Forests and/or TimberWest, the forest company holding Tree Farm License (TFL) #47, as well as several wood-lot licensees. Private landowners are much appreciated for also allowing trails and routes over their land.

---

74. **Cape Mudge:** Captain Vancouver named the cape in 1792 after his first lieutenant on HMS *Discovery*, Zachary Mudge (1770-1852).
75. **Quadra Island** is named after Don Juan Francisco de la Bodega y Quadra, a Spanish naval officer who explored the west coast in 1775 and 1779.

QUADRA ISLAND | 127

Map M20A Quadra Island (Central)

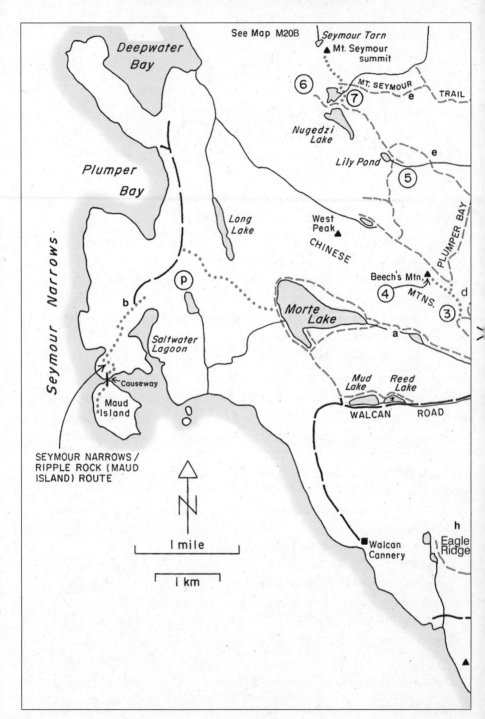

See Map M20B

Seymour Tarn

Mt. Seymour summit

6

MT. SEYMOUR   TRAIL

7   e

Nugedzi Lake

Lily Pond   e

5

West Peak

CHINESE   PLUMPER BAY

Deepwater Bay

Plumper Bay

Long Lake

Beech's Mtn.

4   MTNS.   d

3

Seymour Narrows

b   p

Morte Lake

a

Saltwater Lagoon

Causeway

Maud Island

Mud Lake   Reed Lake

WALCAN   ROAD

SEYMOUR NARROWS / RIPPLE ROCK (MAUD ISLAND) ROUTE

N

1 mile

1 km

Walcan Cannery

h   Eagle Ridge

128

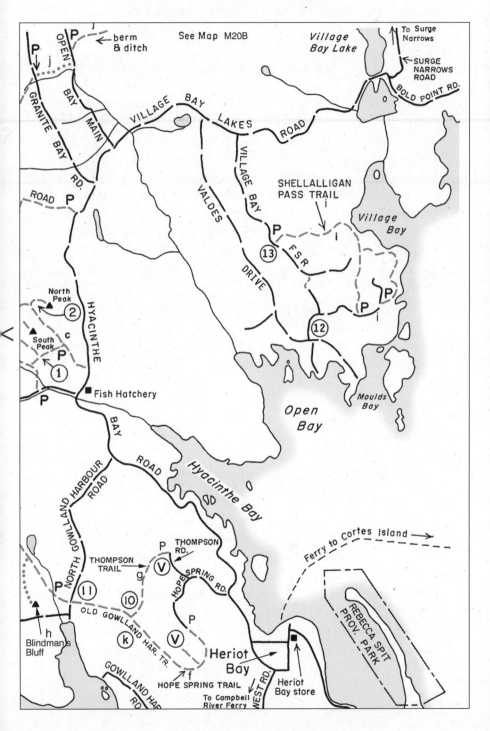

20.a Morte Lake   Map M20A

ACCESS From the Heriot Bay store, take the Hyacinthe Bay Road for 6.1 km to Walcan Road. Turn west (left) along it for 750 m to the Morte Lake parking area.

TRAILS The South Shore Loop is a pleasant forest hike of 7.2 km with good views of Morte Lake, the southwest slopes of the Chinese Mountains and glimpses of the mountains of Vancouver Island. Travelling in a counter-clockwise direction the trail follows a gentle incline above McKercher Creek for 2.3 km to the east end of Morte Lake. Stay to the left at the fork just before (east of) the lake, and follow the trail to a small marshy area by a sandy beach at the southernmost end of the lake. The trail rises again over rocky ridges before dropping steeply to Mud Lake. Mud Lake and Reed Lake sections can be wet. If so, the Walcan Road may be accessed from the west end of each of these lakes. Allow about two hours, return.

The North Shore has the same access, but stay to the right at the fork before Morte Lake and follow the trail around the north side of the lake. This is a strenuous section and the 3 km loop will add about an hour to your hiking time. At the west end of Morte Lake the trail crosses Quadra Conservancy property, private land on Morte Lake purchased by the Quadra community in 1993. The Quadra Island Conservancy and Stewardship Society was formed at this time. Please respect this area by staying on the trail.

20.b Maude Island/Seymour[76] Narrows   Map M20A

DESCRIPTION This is a fairly long and strenuous hike so allow at least five or six hours round-trip from Morte Lake, plus "whirlpool-gazing" time. The Maude Island/Seymour Narrows trail is a pleasant walk through second-growth timber west of Morte Lake, over a steep promontory overlooking the Narrows of Discovery Passage, and finally onto Maude Island where powerline towers carry electricity to Quadra Island and where you can view the swirling currents of the Narrows and the busy marine traffic. Ripple Rock, which once blocked these narrows and was a hazard to shipping, was removed by a huge, controlled blast in 1958, the world's largest non-nuclear explosion. (See also, Section 21.f)

---

76. **Seymour Narrows** was named after Rear Admiral Sir George Francis Seymour, commander of the Pacific Station 1844-1848.

TRAIL The trail/route to Seymour Narrows at Maude Island starts about 100 m west of the outflow creek at Morte Lake. This attractive approach follows an old cat track to the west, descending gradually to a logging road between Saltwater Lagoon and Plumper Bay. As logging progresses from the south, this route might be affected, so make local enquiries before attempting the hike.

Turn left (south) on this logging road. Go about 300 m beyond a rock pit, to a sign for the trail. The trail is the right fork (west) and goes a short distance through an old slide area into the woods. Shortly, a lower return trail joins on the left; ignore this and continue upward to rock bluffs overlooking Saltwater Lagoon and Maude Island. The trail descends steeply from these bluffs to where there is a junction with two signs. Left (east), will be your return trail via Saltwater Lagoon. This is a favourite place for wildlife.

By continuing to the right (southwest) at this fork, the trail to Seymour Narrows skirts above a small bay and then follows an old construction road to a rock causeway leading across to Maude Island. It is interesting to watch water going through the rockfill when the tide is higher on one side than the other. A tidal energy test site is planned for this passage, so the causeway will probably be removed soon, and a structure supporting test turbines will cross to Maude Island. Cross the causeway—or the replacement structure—and once on Maude Island, climb an incline, passing more of the Ripple Rock tunnelling activities, to an excellent viewpoint overlooking Seymour Narrows.

The massive whirlpools and current movement, which at full flood combine in a gentle roar, can be awe-inspiring to watch. Currents here can attain speeds of about 16 knots. Check the time of maximum flow beforehand to see the water running at its fastest. Consult the Canadian Tide and Current Tables, Vol. 6, published by Canadian Hydrographic Service.

20.c Chinese Mountains   Map M20A

DESCRIPTION There are two major peaks; the trail to the North Peak is easier, but the view from the South Peak is far more spectacular with a panorama of the Coast Range, Desolation Sound, the Strait of Georgia and Vancouver Island Mountains. Moss-covered rock ridges and weather-worn stunted growth provide both peaks with a sub-alpine characteristic at about 300 m elevation. The Chinese Mountains area has a particular reputation for ticks, in season. Check carefully after a hike that you haven't gained such an unwanted friend. (See Creatures et al, page 15.)

ACCESS The access road into the Chinese Mountains is 6.7 km from the Heriot Bay store and 600 m north of Walcan Road.

TRAILS To reach the South Peak (327 m) of the Chinese Mountains, from the parking area take the left-hand (southwest) trail around the base of the mountain. After about 500 m keep right, uphill, at the signed fork.① The trail going down is a short connection to the Morte Lake Trail. The path leading to the viewpoint cairn is well marked and, on the ridge, passes a fork that leads down the east side of South Peak, permitting a round trip. Allow two to three hours for this loop.

Alternatively, to reach the South Peak from its east side, take the right-hand (northwest) trail from the parking area up a fairly steep old logging road. At the signed fork,② just where the incline eases, go left to the south summit ridge and join the trail coming up from the west side, continuing to the lookout cairn.

For the North Peak, start as for the South Peak east side (above) but keep straight on where the incline eases.② When reaching the North Peak rock ridge from the trail, take particular note of your surroundings; it is easy to overshoot the trail on the return.

20.d Beech's Mountain   Map M20A

DESCRIPTION This is a fairly strenuous hike, reaching around 500 m in elevation, through old-growth forest and over moss-covered rock bluffs. The constantly unfolding views of the Strait of Georgia, islands and surrounding mountains are spectacular. Allow about four hours return to the Chinese Mountains parking area.

TRAILS For the summit of Beech's Mountain, follow the South Chinese Mountain west side trail (previous section) to a signed fork ③ where the left trail continues to climb steadily in and out of the forest to the 465 m peak.

Beyond Beech's summit, only a route continues along the edge of the ridge towards West Chinese Mountain. The West Peak has some open rock and a ridge-edge scramble. From West Peak there are vistas of the Strait of Georgia and Vancouver Island peaks within Strathcona Provincial Park. However, this trail/route is not maintained and some lines are steep and treacherous.

20.e Mount Seymour   Map M20A

DESCRIPTION Mount Seymour (650 m) is the highest elevation on Quadra Island. Openings in the old-growth provide segmented view-scapes.

ACCESS Follow Hyacinthe Bay Road 9.6 km from the Heriot Bay store and then take the Granite Bay Road for 2 km to Mount Seymour Trail on the left (west). There is parking just beyond this point, on the right.

TRAIL After hiking about 1 km, at a fork bear left (west). After another 1 km, about 100 m before the short connector trail into Little Nugedzi Lake,⑦ a sign marks the start of the route up to the Mount Seymour summit. Follow cairns and flagging, with sharp changes in direction, to the flat bedrock just below the summit. Observe where the trail comes out to find it on your return. Allow four to five hours for the round trip.

DESCRIPTION The Nugedzi Lakes Trail is a 4.25 km trail that begins with a boring 45-minute grunt up an old logging road. However, hikers are well rewarded by the high, mossy and beautiful ancient forest and charming Nugedzi Lakes, especially Little Nugedzi with its bonsai-like islets. The trail was developed by the Quadra Island Recreation Society in conjunction with TimberWest, and is well marked.

ACCESS Take Hyacinthe Bay Road for 9.1 km from the Heriot Bay store, then turn left (west) onto the old Plumper Bay Road (sign-posted as Nugedzi Lakes). The parking area is 100 m up the road.

TRAIL The main trail ascends Plumper Bay Road to a fork where you angle right, reaching the Lily Pond in about 3 km. Turn right at the junction, and hike northwest another 1.5 km to Nugedzi Lake. Allow 4½ hours for a return hike to the lakes.

Beyond Nugedzi Lake another spur trail rises west to a viewpoint ⑥ overlooking Discovery Passage, one hour return from the lake. Along Little Nugedzi's shore there is a boardwalk where naturalists can study the lake/marsh transition zone. At the east end of the boardwalk there is a 500 m link ⑦ to the Mount Seymour Trail. This alternate access to Little Nugedzi Lake, via the Mount Seymour Trail and the short link trail, is actually the preferred route. A spur trail branches from the main route at the Lily Pond, either southeast ⑤ to a lookout (half hour return) or southwest to a route connecting with Plumper Bay Road and Chinese Mountains. Interrupting this route is a fine beaver dam, which can be seen from the remains of the old boardwalk just below.

20.f Hope Spring Trail   Map M20A

From the Heriot[77] Bay store go 1.4 km north on Hyacinthe Bay Road to Hope Spring Road. Turn left, and go approximately 1 km to the end. The trail continues from the driveway at the very end of the road. Look for the sign. It is an easy gradient to the ridge, where a short spur leads to magnificent views towards the Coast Range to the east and the Vancouver Island peaks in the west. Return to the Hope Spring Trail, which continues descending steeply from the ridge west to the Old Gowlland Harbour Trail below.

20.g Thompson Trail   Map M20A

DESCRIPTION The Thompson trail goes up and over Heriot Ridge, linking Old Gowlland Harbour Trail with Thompson Road. Parallel to the cascading creek, it provides a wonderful symphony of sound.

The Thompson trail is a connector that allows you to make a two hour loop including part of Hope Spring trail, Old Gowlland Harbour trail to the fork, (10) and then northeast on the trail to Thompson Road.

TRAIL From the end of Hope Springs Road, hike south on Hope Spring trail, and make two right turns to reach Old Gowlland Harbour trail. At the fork, (10) hike right (northeast) to another fork, right again, (south) and you reach Thompson Road which connects by road with your starting point.

20.h Blindman's Bluff/Eagle Ridge   Map M20A

DESCRIPTION These two trails, accessed off a disused connection between the populated south part of Quadra Island and the Walcan Cannery region, provide viewpoints over Discovery Passage, some magnificent 300-year-old Douglas-fir, wetlands, and habitat for ground-nesting birds. Formerly, a floating bridge made the "link" connection.

ACCESS From Heriot Bay drive north and take the first left off Hyacinthe Bay Road after Lakeburg Road. Drive southwest along this active logging road 2.5 km to the Missing Link sign to the right into Woodlot 1610. You can park here or continue 1.3 km to the trailhead for the two trails. The parking area is also used for access to Old Gowlland Harbour and Thompson trails.

---

77. **Heriot Bay** and Ridge were named after F.L.M. Heriot, a relative of the Commander-in-chief of the Royal Navy Pacific Station.

TRAILS For the Eagle Ridge trail, follow the old Missing Link trail, an old road grade, to a wetland. Cross a stream and climb steadily onto open bluffs with views over Quadra Island and the wetlands below.

For Blindman's Bluff trail, hike south from the trailhead to a viewpoint that appears (from the south) to be a vertical wall of granite, affording views over Quadra and the peaks of Vancouver Island.

20.i Shellalligan Pass   Map M20A

DESCRIPTION The Shellalligan Pass trail passes through two woodlots, and parallels a rocky shoreline with attractive pocket beaches open to the full fetch of Strait of Georgia winds. Wave action can be spectacular. Allow about four hours to complete the full loop on this moderately difficult trail.

ACCESS The trail can be reached from the Village Bay FSR, where there are parking spots and directional signs 2.3 km south of Village Bay Lakes Road, at the point ⑬ where the FSR meets the inland leg of the longer route (see below.)

The west access is from Village Bay Lakes Road, about 4 km along Valdes Drive. Enter a logging road on the left where there is a wood lot and a trail sign.⑫ Drive in here about 1.7 km to the trailhead. There is parking at another trail sign just above a small bay.

TRAIL Hiking the trail counter-clockwise, the Shellalligan Pass Trail goes down to this bay and then follows the shore. After leaving the shoreline, it rises steeply to a signed fork. The short route is to the left (south) and will take about two hours to loop around. It reaches about 60 m in elevation. The full loop route, which climbs as high as 100 m, goes to the right at the signed fork and descends again, passing two more beaches before turning inland to the Village Bay Forest Service Road,⑬ then back to the logging road on which you entered.

20.j Stramberg Lake   Map M20B

DESCRIPTION This route is fairly flat and can offer a tranquil, shaded walk through some old and second-growth forest, along Stramberg Lake's eastern shore, with vistas of Mount Seymour to the west. While a circuit of the lake is possible, it is not recommended due to logging. The hike along the lake to Stramberg Creek (salmon habitat) and the beaver dam,⑧ return, is about two to three hours.

Map M20B Quadra Island (North)

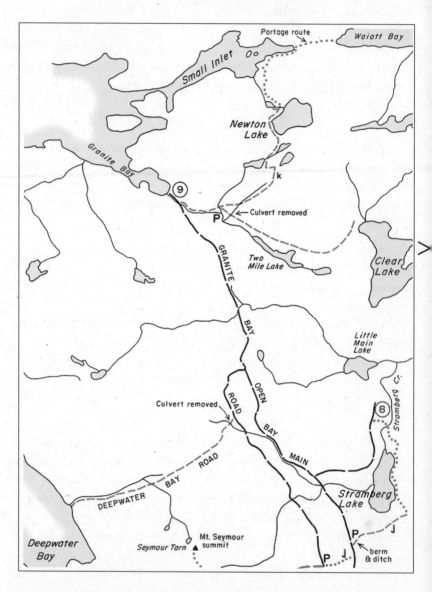

ACCESS Drive north on Hyacinthe Bay Road from Heriot Bay 9.6 km to Granite Bay Road. Continue another 1.2 km north, to the foot of the hill, and turn left (northwest) on Open Bay Main. On this active logging road, go 1.5 km to where an earth berm and a ditch now barricade the old forest road leading towards the lake, where you can park well off the roadway.

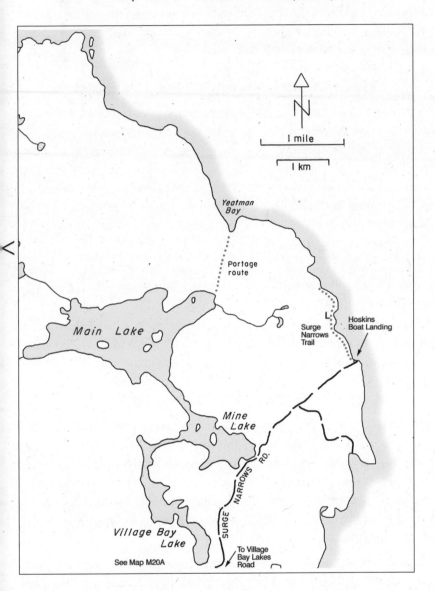

TRAILS: Hike northeast on the old forestry road, bearing left at any forks, to the first view of the lake. An access trail runs down to it here. Go 250 m beyond this point to an old skidder road, sometimes flagged, that leads to the route along the lakeshore. Take this route along the lake to the beaver dam ⑧ across the creek. Return via the same route.

A route links the Mount Seymour Trail with Stramberg Lake. (Refer to Section 20.e) From the trailhead and berm on Open Bay Main, proceed south 300 m and turn right. Follow the north bank of Open Bay Creek, crossing over to Granite Bay Road, about 1 km.

20.k Newton Lake, Small Inlet   Map M20B

DESCRIPTION This hike begins as a fairly easy forest trail, passing other lakes on the way to Newton Lake. Beyond, a more strenuous route follows an old prospectors' trail down to a promontory in Small Inlet, then links with an old portage route (that is sometimes wet) to Waiatt Bay. With only informal consent, this route crosses private property belonging to TimberWest and Merrill & Ring Timber. Please respect this area and do not light fires or camp here. Allow two hours, return, to Newton Lake, or 4½ hours, return, to Waiatt Bay.

ACCESS Follow Granite Bay Road north to within 200 m of Granite Bay, and at the sign ⑨ turn right onto a rough road for 600 m to a fork. Stay left for the trailhead.

The fork to the right is the old logging grade to Clear Lake. This is impassable to vehicles due to a removed culvert but it makes a good hike past Two Mile Lake.

20.l Surge Narrows   Map M20B

DESCRIPTION This is a moderate hike along the shoreline from the end of the road to Surge Narrows Provincial Park. The route is an interesting woods walk and passes beaches, goes over bluffs, and follows ledges above tidal rapids. It offers a mixture of forest and shoreline, with views of islets, whirlpools and wildlife. As at Seymour Narrows, it is worth checking and arranging to be there at maximum flood. Allow two to three hours, return.

ACCESS From the Heriot Bay store take Hyacinthe Bay Road to Village Bay Lakes Road. After crossing the Village Bay Lake bridge, bear left (north) onto Surge Narrows Road and go past Mine Lake. It is 6.2 km from the bridge to the end of the road. Park above the steep incline to the beach. Do not drive down to the water unless you have a four wheel drive vehicle.

TRAIL The route starts from the lower parking area, with flagging on your left as you go down to the boat ramp. Cross the creek via a newly constructed 12 metre footbridge to a small saddle, just on the other (north) side. From here much of the route is a well-trodden path.

The path leads to three main points of interest overlooking Canoe Pass and Surge Narrows. The first of these, which offers the best view of the tidal rapids and islets, is marked with a temporary sign in a large open draw with moss-covered boulders, reached after descending a loose earth sidehill. At times of maximum flood, the difference in water level between the Surge Narrows and the Hoskyn Channel sides can easily be seen from here. Another point of interest is from the bay just to the north. The path continues over a rise, along a ledge above the rapids where there is a 3 m scramble. A fixed rope at this point is helpful.

The third place of interest is a small islet at the south end of Surge Narrows. It is along the shore and around the corner from the north end of this bay and is accessible at low tide. It presents quite a different view of the islands and Beazley Passage. For current and tidal information, refer to the Canadian Tide and Current Tables, Vol. 6, published by the Canadian Hydrographic Service.

Quadra Island view. FRED TRUDELL

21

Campbell River Area

The Campbell River[78] Search and Rescue Society produces their Logging and Highway Road Map, a recreation and logging road guide of the Campbell River region, showing much useful information. This map covers the area north of Strathcona Provincial Park as far as Sayward, and is available at most sporting goods stores. They also publish a similar map extending to the North Coast. (See Map Sources on page 212.) Island Timberlands Recreation and Logging Road Guide to TFL 39 is also useful. (See Logging Companies, page 215.)

21.a Willow Creek Nature Trust   Map 21A

DESCRIPTION The Willow Creek trails provide a beautiful forest and wetland walk along Willow Creek, a salmon enhancement stream and valuable fish habitat. The land comprising Willow Creek Nature Trails (34.2 ha) is held by BC Nature Trust, with stewardship by the Willow Creek Watershed Society.

ACCESS Located at the south end of Campbell River, these trails are accessed from the Highway 19A via Erickson Road and also from Dahl, Martin, Willow Creek or Twillingate roads. You can also come in from the Inland Island Highway (Highway 19) via the Jubilee Parkway and South Dogwood Street.

TRAIL From a parking lot at Erickson Road one trail drops downhill to the stream. Turn east (left) and follow the stream bank to an extension of Martin Road where you cross the stream on a footbridge and return down the other bank. There are many interesting branch trails.

---

78. **Dr. Samuel Campbell** was assistant surgeon on HM survey ship *Plumper,* 1857-1861.

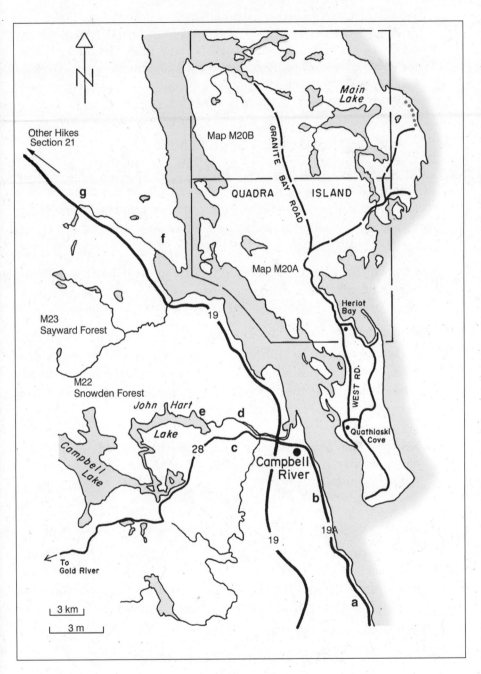

NOTE Along these paths, particularly those near Willow Creek, are great opportunities for bird watching. Look for a variety of woodpeckers, including the red-breasted sapsucker. Many hikers time their visits for viewing seasonal wildflowers and plant life. Improvements include benches, wooden boardwalks and footbridges. Trails can be very wet and muddy in the winter and spring. Leash all pets.

21.b Beaver Lodge Lands   Map 21B

DESCRIPTION This large forestland (415 ha) on the southwest side of Campbell River, adjacent to new subdivisions, is developed by the BCFS for recreation. Trails are multiple-use and accommodate hikers, horses, walkers, runners and mountain bikers. These trails vary in skill level and character, but are mostly "easy" for hikers.

ACCESS: The Beaver Lodge Lands Trails are accessed from Hilchey Road, Rockland Road, South McPhedran Road (with wheelchair access), South Dogwood Street, Trask Road and the Elk River Timber Mainline.

TRAILS The trail along Simms Creek has long been popular, and there are a number of ways to incorporate it into a circular tour from any of the parking areas. The Simms Creek Trail is an even-grade path, providing an easy walk suitable for most users. The trail system provides an interesting diversity of flora and fauna, including swamp life.

NOTES This region is habitat for a variety of wildflowers, birds, and amphibians, even bears and bats. In 1998, the Vancouver Island Butterfly Enthusiasts, sponsored initially by the BCFS and the Canada Trust Friends of the Environment Fund, planted a butterfly garden near Hilchey Road.

Improvements include footbridges and signposts at the trailheads. A kilometre-long fine gravel wheelchair trail can be accessed off South McPhedran Road. Area trails are generally wet and muddy in winter and early spring, though their improved, well-packed surfaces have aided drainage.

21.c Quinsam River   Map 21C

DESCRIPTION The BC Parks Quinsam River Campsite, within Elk Falls Provincial Park and along Highway 28, has drinking water and toilet facilities. The Quinsam River Nature Trail connects with the Canyon

View Trail, near the Quinsam River bridge. From here, follow the south bank of the Campbell River west for 1.2 km to the BC Hydro power station. See Section 21.d.

The Quinsam River Nature trail follows the Quinsam River for 3.3 km to the salmon hatchery. A round trip takes about two hours. It is in good condition and provides an easy walk through a beautiful area. During the spawning season, salmon can be seen returning up the river. For information on the Quinsam Salmon Hatchery contact (250) 287-9564.

The Beaver Pond Trail is an alternative connecting link, about 1 km, between the Quinsam River Nature Trail and the Canyon View Trail.

ACCESS The trailhead is under the Quinsam[79] River Bridge, on Highway 28, about 1.6 km west of the junction of highways 19 and 28, near the Campbell River bridge.

21.d Canyon View Map 21D (also map 21E)

WARNING Water levels in the Campbell River fluctuate due to periodic water release from the John Hart Dam. Loud warning sirens will sound to indicate there is a danger of suddenly rising water. Evacuate the riverbank immediately when you hear the sirens.

No camping or fires are allowed. Obey all warning signs. Use caution and watch for vehicles when hiking across the TimberWest logging road bridge at the east end of trail, and the Quinsam River bridge on Highway 28. The trail is open between 8 am and dusk.

DESCRIPTION The Canyon View Trail was built in 1991 with the support of BC Parks, BC Hydro, Campbell River Lions Club, TimberWest, Ministry of Transportation and Highways, Pacific Coast Energy and the community of Campbell River. Canyon View Trail also provides access to Elk Falls, upstream from the John Hart Generating Station.

ACCESS From the junction of Highways 19 and 28, near the Campbell River bridge, drive west 2.3 km towards Gold River on Highway 28. At the bottom of the big hill swing right, to BC Hydro's John Hart Generating Station and follow the signs to the visitor parking area. Keep out of sign-posted restricted-access areas. There are toilets, a picnic day-use area and several viewing platforms.

---

79. *Quinsam* means "resting place" in the language of the Comox people.

Map M21A Willow Creek Trails

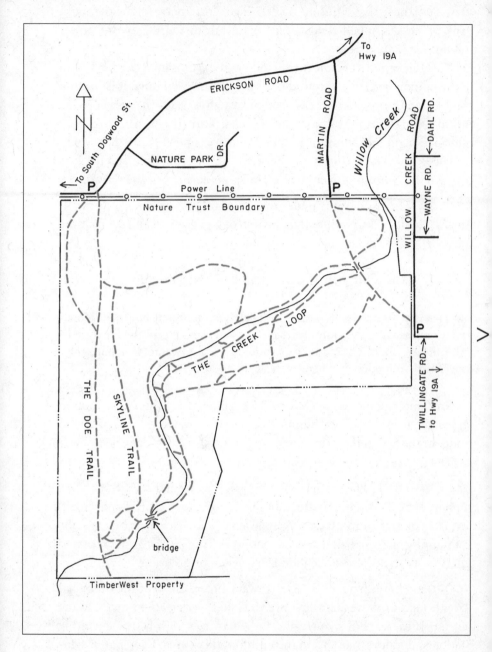

Map M21B Beaver Lodge Trails

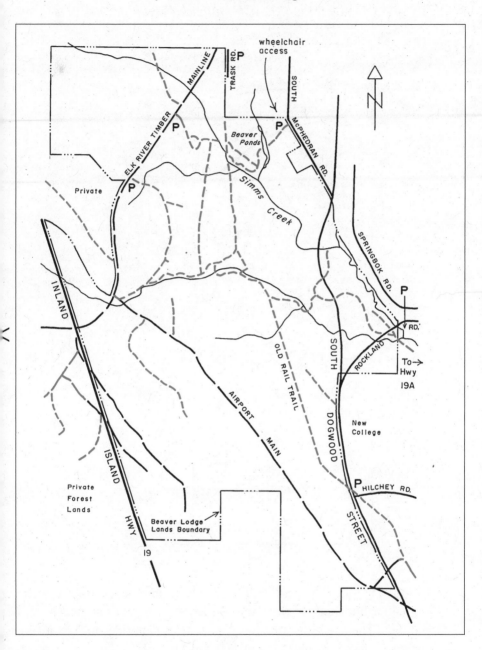

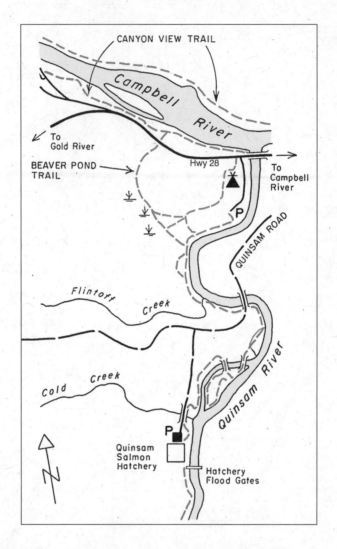

TRAILS On the Canyon View Trail you can complete a 6 km, two-hour loop along both sides of the Campbell River. There are some steep steps and hills. The river is crossed twice: once via a footbridge in the canyon, and again via the TimberWest logging road bridge, farther downstream. A highlight is the canyon footbridge, 24.4 m long, that hides the natural gas pipeline underneath.

The Millennium Trail, beginning near the canyon footbridge, runs 2.5 km along the south side of Campbell River and connects the Canyon

View Trail with the Elk Falls viewpoint. See Section 21.e. The steeper sections are closer to the John Hart Generating Station where there are several long series of steps.

> **NOTE** The Campbell River was officially designated a BC Heritage River in March 2000. The Campbell River and the Quinsam River are on the Outdoor Recreation Council's list of BC's endangered steelhead rivers.

21.e Elk Falls Provincial Park   Map 21E

ACCESS Trails at Elk Falls Provincial Park (1087 ha) are accessed from Highway 28, about 6.5 km west of its junction with Highway 19, near Campbell River. Turn off the highway at the top of General Hill, right, onto Brewster Lake Road, cross a wooden bridge to a fork in the road. The road to the left provides a view of the dam. The road to the right goes to a parking lot that overlooks the falls; the road on the left features groves of big timber.

TRAIL The main trail is approximately 2 km long, is quite steep in some sections, and can be slippery during rainy periods. It takes about 45 minutes for a round trip. There are several different access trails between the parking areas and the river. Stay away from the canyon's sheer cliffs.

The trail follows the Campbell River from Moose Falls to Elk Falls, providing a beautiful walk through an area with gigantic Douglas-fir and cedar trees, some of which are 800 years old, and views of the numerous pools along the river course. The lookout provides a scenic view of Elk Falls, where the water tumbles some 25 m into Elk Falls canyon. The Millennium Trail links this area with the Canyon View Trail.

21.f Ripple Rock
Map 21F (also map 20A)

DESCRIPTION Midway between the lookout at Wilfred Point and Maude Island, off Quadra Island, is the site of the infamous Ripple Rock, two menacing rock pinnacles whose summits used to provide only a few metres clearance at low tide. This notorious marine hazard caused damage to dozens of ships and claimed 114 lives, resulting in a project to destroy Ripple Rock by blowing it to pieces. At that time, April 5, 1958, the largest man-made, non-nuclear explosion in history reduced the rock by 370,000 tonnes to create a clearance of 13 m. In 1984, a cruise ship was

Map M21D   Canyon View

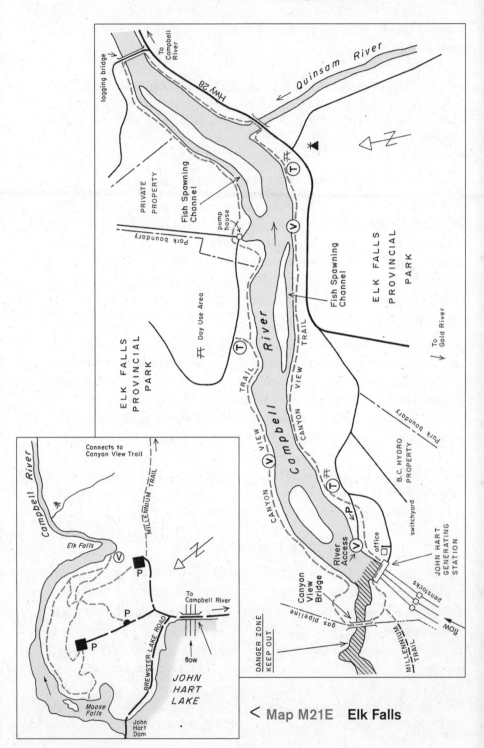

Quinsam River

Hwy 28

To Campbell River

logging bridge

PRIVATE PROPERTY

Fish Spawning Channel

pump house

Park boundary

Day Use Area

Fish Spawning Channel

ELK FALLS PROVINCIAL PARK

To Gold River

N

Campbell River

CANYON VIEW TRAIL

CANYON VIEW TRAIL

ELK FALLS PROVINCIAL PARK

Park boundary

B.C. HYDRO PROPERTY

switchyard

River Access

office

Canyon View Bridge

JOHN HART GENERATING STATION

penstocks

flow

gas pipeline

DANGER ZONE KEEP OUT

MILLENNIUM TRAIL

Connects to Canyon View Trail

MILLENNIUM TRAIL

Campbell River

Elk Falls

Moose Falls

BREWSTER LAKE ROAD

To Campbell River

flow

JOHN HART LAKE

John Hart Dam

< Map M21E   Elk Falls

holed off Maude Island and, although it limped south to Duncan Bay, it sank at the dock.

At the lookout there are views across to Quadra and Maude islands and to the swirling waters below. The trail was constructed in 1983 through a grant sponsored by the Campbell River Rotary Club. Along the route, you pass through areas that were logged about 70 years ago and now have stands of Douglas-fir, red alder, broadleaf maple and western hemlock. On the east side of Menzies Creek the trail passes through two small patches of old-growth with 300 year old Sitka spruce and Douglas-fir. There are good viewpoints along the trail and a nice sandy beach at Nymphe Cove.

ACCESS/TRAIL The marked trailhead is 17 km north of the Campbell River bridge, near the junction of Highways 19 and 28. The sign-posted parking area is on the east side of Highway 19. The trail is 4 km long, with an easy-to-moderate grade to Menzies[80] Bay and a steep section to Wilfred Point. The trail to headland above the former Ripple Rock is a 1½ to 2 hour hike (one way) leading to the Seymour Narrows.

21.g Menzies Mountain   Map 21G

DESCRIPTION The strenuous 3 km Menzies Mountain Trail is somewhat rocky and has steep sections. It provides spectacular views in all directions, especially of the Sayward Forest and the mountains of Vancouver Island. Allow at least two hours, return, from the indicated parking area, more if bad road conditions require you to park lower down and trudge up the logging road.

ACCESS The road to Menzies Mountain is off Highway 19, just over 24 km from the junction of Highway 19 and Highway 28 in Campbell River. The turnoff is on the east side of Highway 19. If there is active logging in the area, the road can be driven as far as the second lookout, although caution should be taken during work hours and right-of-way given to logging trucks. This is a narrow gravel road without many pullouts and there are numerous, confusing side roads. The upper stretches are rough and require a high-slung four wheel drive vehicle. The parking area has room for four or five vehicles.

---

80. **Archibald Menzies** (1754-1842) was a surgeon on Captain Vancouver's ship *Discovery*, but he was also a botanist, with his name appended to plant names, notably the *Arbutus menziesii*.

Map M21G Menzies Mountain

Map M21F Ripple Rock

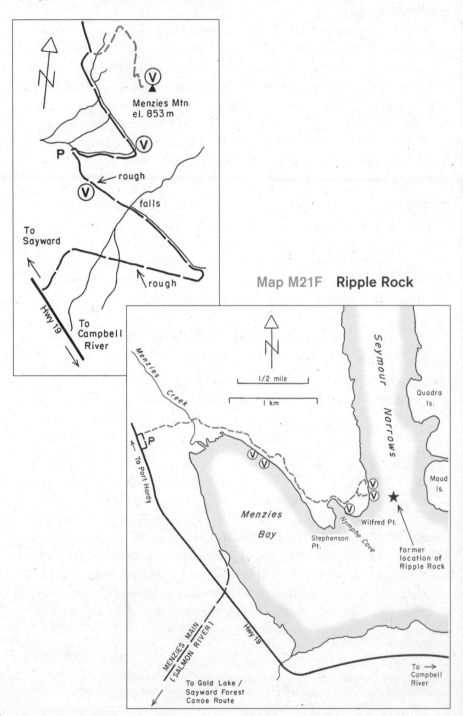

21.h McNair Lake (not on our maps)

The McNair Lake Trail, near the northwest end of Roberts Lake, winds 1.8 km west along a logging road to McNair Lake. This is a popular mountain-biking area. Watch for the trailhead on the left (west) side of Highway 19, about 32.5 km north of the Highway 19 and Highway 28 junction near the Campbell River bridge.

21.i Salmon Lookout (not on our maps)

The Salmon Lookout Trail is approximately 50.5 km north of the Highway 19 and Highway 28 junction in Campbell River. The trail climbs sharply for 3 km to an old forestry lookout and spectacular vista of the Salmon River Valley. Allow two hours for the return trip.

21.j Dalrymple Creek (not on our maps)

Just 9 km east of the Sayward Junction, or around 55.5 km north of the Highway 19 and Highway 28 junction in Campbell River, is the Dalrymple Creek Recreation Trail. From the small parking area on the north (right) side of Highway 19, visitors can enjoy an easy 0.5 km forest walk through private Island Timberlands forestlands.

21.k H'Kusam Mountain Map M21K

DESCRIPTION This is a steep climb in a wilderness environment so carry adequate mountain hiking gear. There are plenty of breath-taking vistas so do not forget your camera. The highlight is an expansive view over the Sayward Valley. Building the trail is a labour of love for Bill West-Sells and his helpers which is why it is known locally as Bill's Trail. See Notes, below, about the *Kusam Klimb*. Contact Bill at (250) 282 3818 for more information or to volunteer to help.

TRAIL From the dogleg up Sabre Road in Sayward, follow signs to the start of the trail and parking. The trail is wide to Cottonwood Loop, where you stay left, and to about 425 m, where it is steep and narrow. Continue until you reach Keta View Rock at 1270 m. There are ropes to assist on the steep parts, but do not rely on them for safety. Along the climb up there are some side trails to lookouts and a rough trail (left) to Springer Peak.

The trail, now gentler, bears right towards the lake past Springer Peak trail (signed), then reaches an open rock bluff where a col and lake are seen, with spectacular views of the Sayward Valley below. Descend steeply to the alpine lake, then climb through open meadows to the col. A round trip on the main trail to the col is about 11 km and takes about six hours. (Over the col, the trail goes down steeply into the Stowe Creek valley. To your left is Stowe Peak. There, you should see *Kusam Klimb* equipment and a trail log box.)

From the col, climb south on a steep and sometimes narrow ridge, exposed in some places, to a meadow, with H'Kusam summit across a gully to the east. Pass two peaks on the right and scramble to the 1670 m summit.

ALTERNATE ACCESS A possibly easier option to climb H'Kusam is to approach via the Stowe Trail. From the short bridge on the highway over Stowe Creek, find Timber Road across from the Mennonite Church. Drive through Dyer Logging camp, the old gate, and straight up the hill. On a rough road, drive 6.4 km. Then ford Stowe Creek and round a steep rough switchback to a parking area at 610 m.

Over the little gate, hike on a wide trail, past *Lyle's Route*, which can be your return option. Continue right up Stowe Trail to a log bridge and shelter, and from here towards the col. Near a waterfall, at a sign, trail log

Sayward Valley from H'Kusam Peak.   BILL WEST-SELLS

Map M21K   H'Kusam Mountain

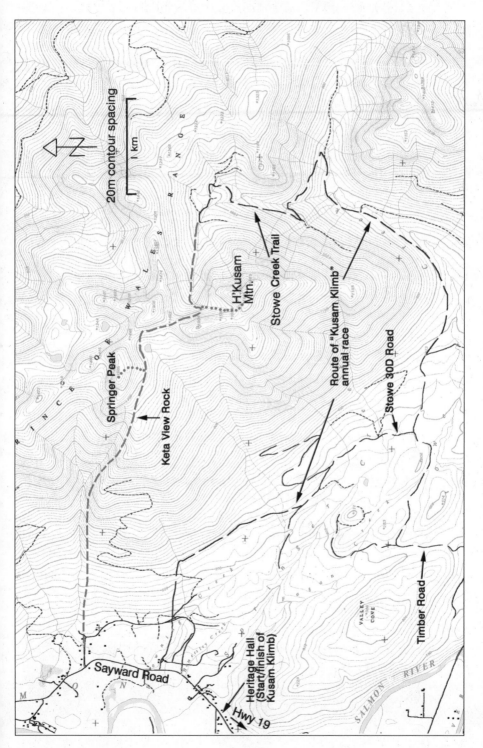

20m contour spacing

1 km

H'Kusam Mtn.

Stowe Creek Trail

Route of "Kusam Klimb" annual race

Stowe 30D Road

Springer Peak

Keta View Rock

Timber Road

Sayward Road

Heritage Hall (Start/finish of Kusam Klimb)

Hwy 19

SALMON RIVER

VALLEY CONE

153

box and large rope, climb straight up and left to the top of the waterfall. Drop into the big V-shaped creek bed above the waterfall and follow this creek past some huge boulders and then left around a thick stunted forest into a bowl, often full of snow. To your left is the shorter and possibly easier route to the summit.

> **NOTES** The *Kusam Klimb*, which runs in late June, has become a major running endurance event. Competitors climb to the col, and go down into the Stowe Valley, and return via mostly deactivated logging roads, a total of 23 km.

21.I Mount Kitchener   Map M21L

DESCRIPTION This trail ascends to the lower (southern) summit of Mount Kitchener on the southern end of the Prince of Wales Range and then across to the middle summit. The higher main summit is close by but it is not recommended for the average hiker. Great views appear over Johnstone Strait to West Thurlow Island. To the east of the summit is the site of a plane crash.

ACCESS Turn off Hwy 19 onto the Bigtree Main just before crossing Bigtree Creek. Take the first road on the right, just before the creek crossing, and follow that northeast and again take the first right. This road swings up onto the southwest ridge of Mount Kitchener. There is a left switchback marked by a cairn. Follow it to the end, marked by a downed tree with many ribbons, where there is room to turn around and park.

TRAIL: The trail begins on the uphill side of the road at about the 1100 m level and scrambles through logging slash for a couple of minutes before entering the old growth forest. The obvious trail gently climbs for two hundred and fifty metres until it breaks out onto rocky benches in the alpine. It is then a short scramble up to the southern summit. To reach the middle summit drop back down onto the heather bench and then descend forty metres to a saddle. There is no defined trail to reach the middle summit but there may be flagging in place.

> **NOTES** There is a gate on the Bigtree Main just after leaving the highway but it is rarely locked. However, watch for logging trucks. This is an easy day trip and from the end of the road to the south summit takes about two hours.

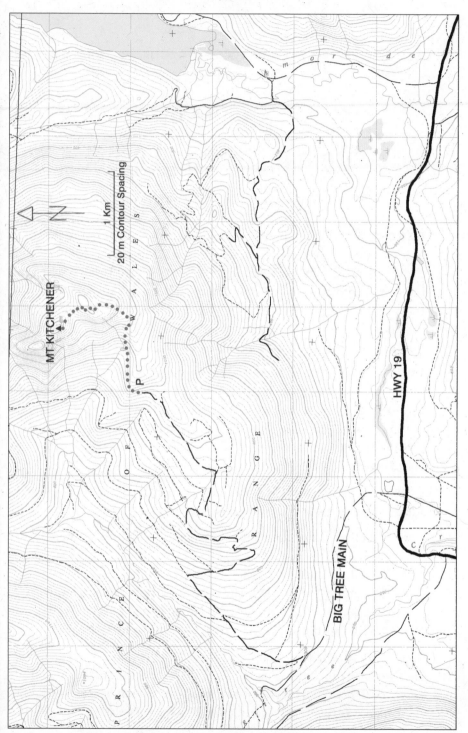

MT KITCHENER

P

W A L E S

O F

R A N G E

P R I N C E

N

1 Km

20 m Contour Spacing

HWY 19

BIG TREE MAIN

22

Snowden
Demonstration Forest

DESCRIPTION The Snowden Demonstration Forest was designed to raise public awareness about Integrated Resource Management in provincial forests. In this "active" forest, silvicultural systems are integrated with other forest interests including recreation. A system of trails in this area, while perhaps not for those who prefer alpine hiking, provides a variety of interpretive and recreational forest-based opportunities suitable for all ages. Mountain bikes are allowed on the trails.

ACCESS This area is just outside Campbell River. From the junction of Highways 19 and 28 near the Campbell River bridge, follow Highway 28 about 6.5 km toward Gold River. At the top of the big hill (General Hill) take the right turn onto Brewster Lake Road, heading to Elk Falls Provincial Park. At the sign for Loveland Bay stay left and cross the John Hart Dam. Follow the directional signs from there.

INTERPRETIVE TRAILS Three hiking trails are located on Snowden Road on the west side of the Demonstration Forest.

- Old Forest Trail: 325 m long, a 15-minute walk through an old growth forest.
- Ecosystem Trail: 800 m, shows examples of forest ecology.
- Silviculture Trail: 1.1 km. The complete forest management cycle is examined, from site preparation to planting, tending and harvesting.

Check with the BCFS Campbell River District office about the availability of area brochures. The BCFS originally constructed 40 km of trails here. Local mountain bike clubs have built over 60 km of routes. A biker's route map is available at several Campbell River bike stores.

Sayward Forest, water and wilderness   RICHARD BLIER

RECREATIONAL TRAILS Numerous trails provide opportunities for hiking, cycling, running and mushroom picking.

- Old Rail Trail ⑤⑴ runs 4.2 km along a historical rail grade. The trail head is located north of Elmer Lake on the Frog Lake Road.
- Lookout Loop ⑤⑵ is a 3.2 km loop that starts from the Frog Lake Road, climbing up and over rocky outcrops, then down through forest and wetland areas. It joins up with the Old Rail Trail.
- Enchanted Forest ⑤⑶ near Elmer Lake, is 4.3 km long, through lush forest and along rough gravel roads. Cyclists are recommended to ride this loop in a clockwise direction.
- Riley Lake Connector ⑤⑷ runs for 1.9 km of forest trail and old rail grade that connects Enchanted Forest and Lost Lake Trails. Head-banger Hookup is a parallel route, principally for cyclists.
- Lost Lake Trail ⑤⑸ is a 5.5 km loop with picnic tables at the south end of the lake. There is a short hike to a rocky viewpoint near the north end of the loop.
- Mudhoney Pass ⑤⑹ is an extension of this trail, principally for cyclists.
- The Lost Frog ⑤⑺ includes 8.2 km of almost-continuous rail grade, with a few rougher connections. Access to the south end of the trail is via the north end of Devlin Road, or to the north via Frog Lake Road. The Frog Lake Road,⑤⑻ 5.7 km, is an optional link between Frog Lake and Lost Lake trail systems.

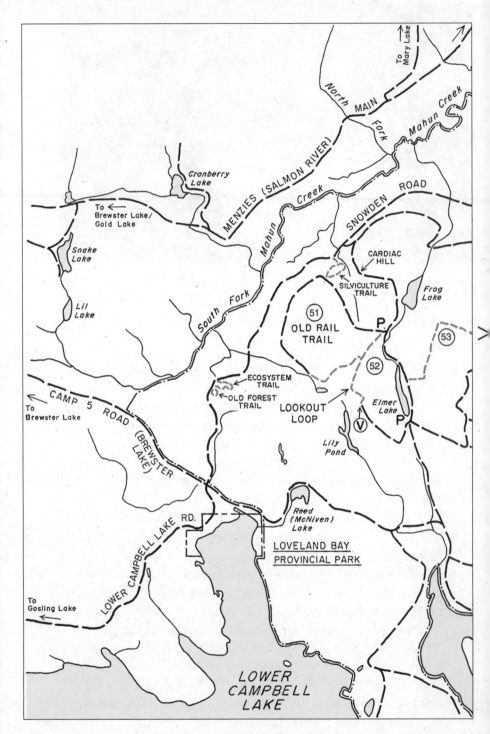

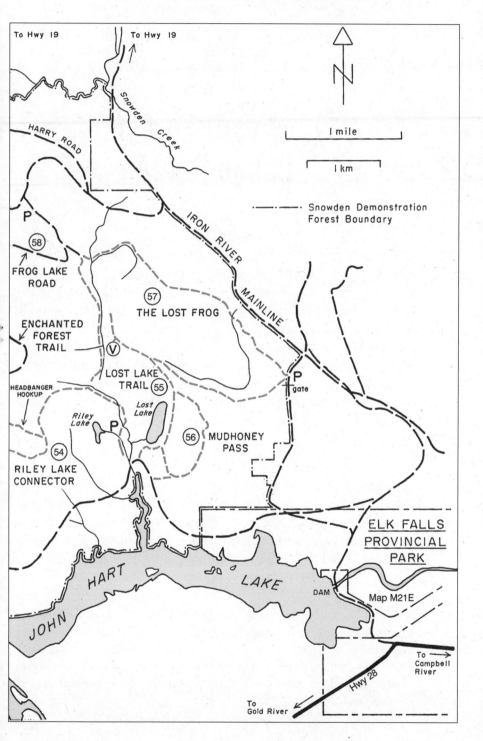

To Hwy 19

To Hwy 19

N

Snowden Creek

HARRY ROAD

IRON RIVER MAINLINE

1 mile

1 km

Snowden Demonstration Forest Boundary

P

58
FROG LAKE ROAD

57
THE LOST FROG

ENCHANTED FOREST TRAIL

V

LOST LAKE TRAIL 55

HEADBANGER HOOKUP

Riley Lake

Lost Lake

P

P
gate

56 MUDHONEY PASS

54
RILEY LAKE CONNECTOR

ELK FALLS PROVINCIAL PARK

JOHN HART LAKE

DAM

Map M21E

Hwy 28

To → Campbell River

To Gold River

23

Sayward Forest
Canoe Route

DESCRIPTION The Sayward Forest was named after William Parsons Sayward, a pioneer logger and sawmill operator. The terrain is undulating, largely covered with immature and some maturing second-growth timber. There are numerous lakes and creeks. In 1938 a large forest fire burned much of the area. The forest was subsequently replanted and today this is the most intensively managed forest in BC.

The BCFS has developed rustic recreation sites throughout the area in conjunction with a continuous canoe and portage route. The Sayward Forest Canoe Route is approximately 40 km in length and includes about 7 km of portages, recently upgraded and widened. Most of these lake links accommodate canoes that are portaged on wheels. A circuit of this eleven-lake system takes most canoeists about three to four days.

ACCESS The Sayward Forest Canoe Route is best accessed at Morton Lake Provincial Park. From the junction of Highways 19 and 28 near the Campbell River bridge, keep north on Highway 19. Drive 14.5 km to the Island Timberlands Menzies Bay (Salmon River) Mainline. Swing west on the mainline and continue 9.5 km west to the park access road. From here it is about 6.5 km to Morton Lake.

NOTE Check with Island Timberlands North Division for updates on truck hauling, road conditions and access restrictions. (See timber companies, Appendix.) Contact the BCFS Campbell River District office about the availability of a canoe route brochure giving route details and safety precautions. See map M23 for other vehicle access points to the canoe loop.

Map M23   Sayward Forest

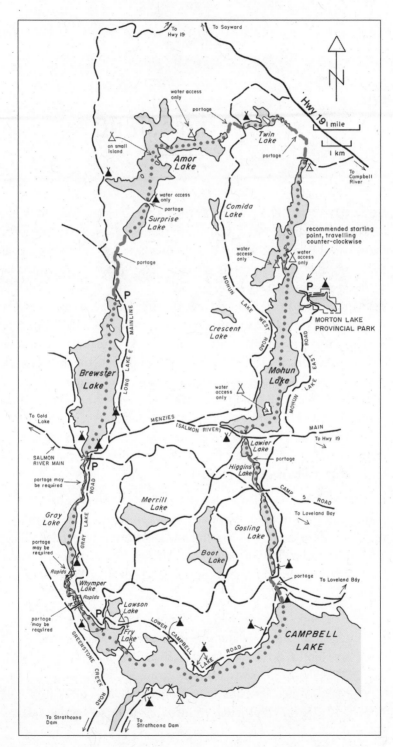

24

Nootka Island

DESCRIPTION The Nootka Trail is a remote, unpatrolled wilderness destination. The Nootka Trail does not exist—at least, not officially. However, this rugged 35 km route along Nootka Island's west coast has been travelled for thousands of years. The village of Yuquot is at least 4,300 years old. It was here, in 1778, that the Nu-chah-nulth people greeted Captain Cook and his crew, the first Europeans on the west coast.

The Nootka Trail is mostly on Crown Land and falls within a Special Management Zone, a category that recognizes the region's intrinsic wilderness and historical importance, yet does not save the area from future development. The old-growth trail from Louie Bay Lagoon to Third Beach is not protected. The Land Use Plan's buffer zone is only 200 m in width, while, in places, the trail extends inland much farther than that. Future development and leasing for recreation and rural purposes could occur on several tracts of private land. That possibility, and area logging, could impact the wilderness experience.

ACCESS The normal start for hikers is at the trail's north end. Float-planes can land in Louie Bay Lagoon, where visitors disembark, usually into knee-deep water. (Shorts and sandals are recommended.) There are several operators, both air and water, to get you to the north end of the trail and/or to the south termination of the trail at Yuquot, or Friendly Cove.

- Air Nootka provides flights to Louie Bay, the cost varies depending upon the number of passengers, weight, etc.
  Air Nootka, Box 19, Gold River, BC, V0P 1G0
  (250) 283-2255, www.airnootka.com.
- Maxi's Water Taxi, Box 1122, Gold River, BC, V0P 1G0
  (250) 283-2282, provides connections for hikers and kayakers

between Gold River and Yuquot/Friendly Cove. Weather permitting you can arrange a water taxi to Louie Bay. The boat is a 12-passenger Coast Guard approved vessel.
- The MV Uchuck III offers passenger and freight service to Yuquot/ Friendly Cove and Gold River between mid-June and late September. Nootka Sound Service, (M.V. Uchuck III) Box 57, Gold River, BC, V0P 1G0 (250) 283-2515, www.mvuchuck.com.

The Nootka Trail terminates at Yuquot/Friendly Cove. There is a $5.00 fee to cross the First Nations land and visit the historical museum, a former church. Only one family remains at Yuquot. The other Mowachaht Band members moved to the Gold River area in 1968. You can camp near Yuquot or rent one of six small cabins.

For more information contact: Mowachaht/Muchalaht First Nation Band Office, Box 459, Gold River, BC, V0P 1G0 (250) 283-2335; 1-800-238-2933 (toll-free); or fax (250) 283-2335; e-mail: info@yuquot.ca.

The dock at Yuquot accommodates floatplanes, the MV Uchuck III out of Gold River, and a water taxi service. The nearby Friendly Cove lighthouse still has a lightkeeper. Santa Gertrudis-Boca Del Infierno Provincial Marine Park (440 ha) protects a coastal marine environment and an old-growth forest, north of Friendly Cove. The park can be accessed only by water. The bay is a sheltered anchorage for paddlers and boaters.

TRAIL/ROUTE A rugged trail leads south of Louie Bay Lagoon through an old-growth forest to Third Beach. This is the roughest part of the hike. At beautiful Third Beach you will discover an expansive sandy beach where there is camping and water. Hiking time from Louie Bay Lagoon to Third Beach is about an hour.

You can day-hike northwest from Third Beach to a saltwater narrows at Louie Bay's south end. This waterway is passable only at tides of 1.8 m or less. Tidal information is crucial here and all along the Nootka Trail, to avoid being trapped by high tides.

From the narrows, head north along the mudflats to Tongue Point. Here you will find the remains of a hull from a wrecked ship, moved here as part of an unsuccessful salvage operation. The Greek ship Tries Ierarchi smashed into the rocks in late 1969, southeast of Ferrer Point. If time and tides are in your favour, you can consider following a somewhat overgrown road from Tongue Point to Northwest Cone where there are the ruins of an early radar installation. Estimated one-way hiking times:

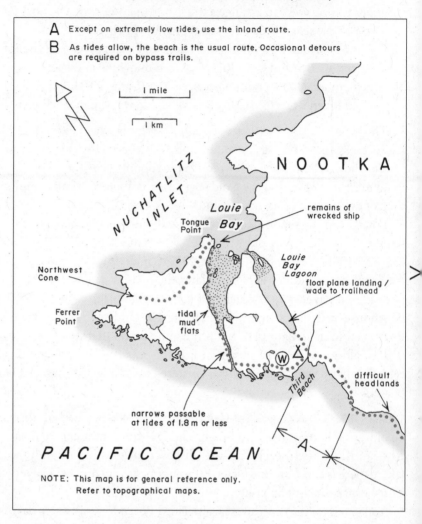

A Except on extremely low tides, use the inland route.

B As tides allow, the beach is the usual route. Occasional detours are required on bypass trails.

1 mile

1 km

NUCHATLITZ INLET

NOOTKA

Louie Bay

Tongue Point

remains of wrecked ship

Louie Bay Lagoon

float plane landing / wade to trailhead

Northwest Cone

Ferrer Point

tidal mud flats

Third Beach

difficult headlands

narrows passable at tides of 1.8 m or less

PACIFIC OCEAN

NOTE: This map is for general reference only.
Refer to topographical maps.

Third Beach to the narrows, one hour; the narrows to Tongue Point, one hour; Tongue Point to Northwest Cone, one hour.

Starting south from Third Beach, the Nootka Trail cuts inland to avoid a tricky headland about 1 km to the southeast. Watch for floats and buoys hanging in the trees at the start of the bypass route. The beach route is passable only on an extreme low tide. South of the headland, hike along the tidal shelf to Skuna Bay, where you will find good camping and water.

Another tricky beach passage is just before Calvin Creek. Calvin Creek empties Crawfish and Ewart lakes. Calvin Falls, 6 m high, is a trail

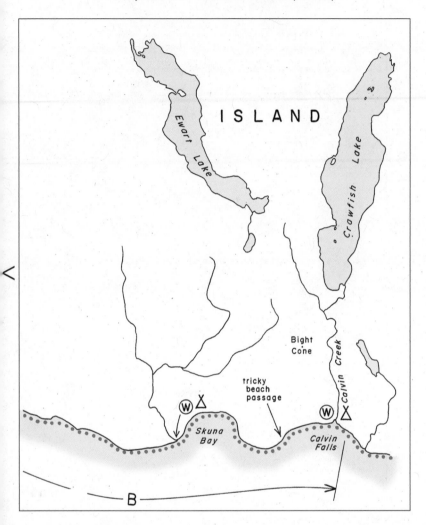

highlight. There is good camping and water here. Estimated hiking time from Third Beach to Calvin Falls is 4 or 5 hours.

The beach is the usual route from Calvin Falls to Beano Creek. South of the falls the trail crosses Bajo Creek, an unreliable water source due to its brackish nature. Bajo Point is a First Nations Reserve and an ancient village site, once known as E'as. Respect this private land. From the point you can watch for whales and sea otters. By the mid-1800s, the indigenous otters had been depleted by early fur trading, mainly Russian. The sea otter was successfully re-introduced to the area, over 30 years ago.

Map M24B   Nootka Island (South)

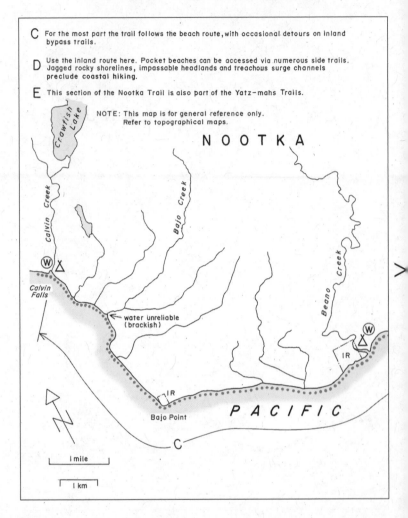

C For the most part the trail follows the beach route,with occasional detours on inland bypass trails.

D Use the inland route here. Pocket beaches can be accessed via numerous side trails. Jagged rocky shorelines, impassable headlands and treachous surge channels preclude coastal hiking.

E This section of the Nootka Trail is also part of the Yatz-mahs Trails.

NOTE: This map is for general reference only. Refer to topographical maps.

Crowfish Lake

N O O T K A

Calvin Creek

Bajo Creek

Beano Creek

W △

Calvin Falls

← water unreliable (brackish)

W △

IR

IR

Bajo Point

P A C I F I C

C

1 mile

1 km

At Beano Creek there is camping and water. The ancient whaling village of Tsarksis was located nearby. The tricky crossing at Beano Creek is easiest at low tide. Approximate hiking time from Calvin Falls to Beano Creek is 3 to 4 hours.

To avoid impassable headlands and surge channels, hikers are forced onto the inland trail, just north of Callicum Creek. There is camping and water on the beach near the creek mouth. Fill up your water here, as this is the last reliable source until you reach a small beach near Yuquot. The inland trail runs along the cliffs and is somewhat exposed. Pocket beaches can be accessed via challenging side trails. Drop your packs at the

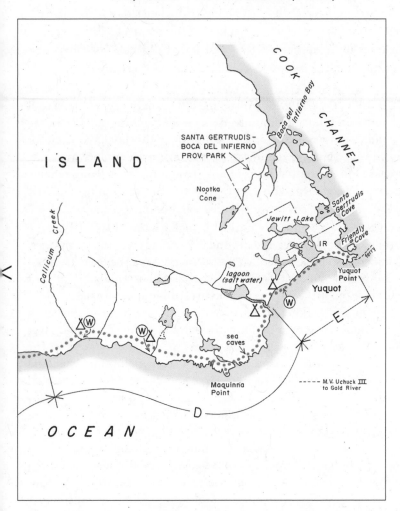

side of the main trail and take a short 10 minute walk to Maquinna Point and a spectacular seascape. Under a kilometre south of Maquinna Point, a shore access route drops down to a beach with three sea caves.

There is good swimming at the narrows where a tidal saltwater river flows in and out of Tsa'tsil Lagoon. It is a formidable torrent at times, but traversable and not very deep at low tide. You can camp here, best on the southwest side, but there is no water. The next spot for camping and water is a pocket beach to the east. Allow at least 8 or 9 hours hiking time between Beano Creek and the tidal lagoon. Many hikers make this a two-day stretch.

The trail between the tidal lagoon and Yuquot, part of Yatz-mahs Trails, is maintained by the Mowachaht/Muchalat Band, the Ministry of Forests, and Western Forest Products. Other trails lead through old-growth trees to an unnamed lake and Jewitt (Aa-aak-quaksius) Lake. Hiking time from the lagoon to Yuquot is around 1.5 hours.

NOTES AND CAUTIONS Hikers must be experienced with coastal travel and geared for extreme adverse weather conditions. Refer to the Hints and Cautions section at the beginning of this book. Gear up for wilderness conditions and allow at least four or five days for your hike. Be prepared for torrential rains at any time of the year. Bring reliable raingear and a good tent with a waterproof fly. Pack everything in plastic bags. Use waterproof covers for your pack and sleeping gear.

Carry and use a compass. Consider bringing a portable VHF marine radio for receiving weather updates and for sending emergency messages. Many hikers also pack a small GPS. Precise tidal knowledge is essential when hiking the Nootka Trail. Use the Canadian Tide and Current Tables, Vol. 6, published by the Canadian Hydrographic Service.

Start your day's hiking on a falling tide. Many sections of the beach route are impassable on a flooding or high tide. Some creek and river crossings are only safe at low tide. Floats, buoys and markers in the shoreline trees indicate inland trails, beach access points and headland bypass routes. Watch for irregular, large and dangerous rogue waves, particularly if you are hiking the shelves and around headlands. As for tsunamis, in some places you will have to take the remote risk. When camping, set up your tent well above the high tide line.

The trail traverses a variety of shoreline that includes sandy, pebbled and boulder beaches, slippery, seaweed-covered tidal zones, slick sandstone shelves, irregular peninsulas and rocky ledges. Sections of the inland trail can be extremely muddy. Blowdowns may impede the route. A 15 m rope may be required on some headland bypass trails.

Boil, treat or filter all water. Availability is dependent on the season and weather. Be careful and sparing with fires. Use a small stove whenever possible. Choose your campsite carefully to lessen area impact and prevent the contamination of water sources. Hang your food away from camp. Bears and wolves inhabit the area.

Check with the Department of Fisheries about possible red tide (paralytic shellfish poisoning, or PSP) alerts, permanently closed areas, and spot closures before consuming shellfish. For updates visit www.pac. dfo-mpo.gc.ca. The 24-hour DFO information line is (604) 666-2828 or 1-800-465-4336 (toll-free).

MAPS AND GUIDES The two topographical maps for the Nootka Trail are NTS 92E/10 Nootka (1:50,000) (which covers the entire trail except the northern tip) and NTS 92E/5 Zeballos (1:50,000) (which shows the trail's north end). Pal Horvath's *The Nootka Trail: A Backpacker's Guide*, is a concise guide to the Nootka Trail. The booklet has a small-scale general map, contains 13 colour photos, and is filled with camping hints, hiking highlights and descriptions of side routes that a dozen trips along the trail have revealed. Contact (250) 285-2357 for more information.

The Federation of Mountain Clubs of BC (FMCBC) publishes an excellent Nootka Trail brochure and map. This informative pamphlet, spearheaded by members of the Alpine Club of Canada (ACC), British Columbia Mountaineering Club (BCMC) and Comox District Mountaineering Club (CDMC), has been instrumental in publicizing the Nootka Trail. Contact them at 130 West Broadway, Vancouver, BC V5Y 1P3. Phone (604) 873-6096 or visit www.mountainclubs.org. For tidal information consult Canadian Tide and Current Tables, Vol. 6, published by the Canadian Hydrographic Service, and available at marine and sporting goods stores.

SCHOEN LAKE AND Mt SCHOEN

25

Schoen Lake
Provincial Park

DESCRIPTION Schoen[81] Lake is in the centre of a remote wilderness area and the access to several hiking routes, some of which are used to climb Mount Schoen. There has been no trail work, so the routes are often overgrown and route-finding is very difficult, although there are some remnant flags and sections of obvious trail. The small BC Provincial Park campsite, located at the west end of Schoen Lake, has services provided by a Park Facility Operator. Overnight fees, charged between May 15th and September 30th, are $10.00 per party per night (2008).

ACCESS Refer to Western Forest Products recreational pamphlet and maps M25 and M26. For the Schoen Lake Provincial Park (8689 ha), head west on Highway 19 from the Sayward Junction. Drive 54.5 km toward Woss and then watch for the Mount Cain/Schoen Lake sign-posted turnoff, just beyond Croman Lake. Turn left onto Davie Road and follow the Park signs another 14 km to the campground. If travelling from Woss, turn right about 10.5 km east of Woss onto Davie Road. The Davie River addition (259 ha) protects old-growth forest on a steep ridge visible as you approach the park from Highway 19. The area is important habitat for elk and deer.

Around 5 km from the Highway 19 cut-off you will reach a junction. To the left is the access road up to Mount Cain Regional Park, described in Section 26. The road to Schoen Lake, not recommended for large RVs, becomes rougher as you near the campsite. At Schoen Lake you will find nine developed campsites and a striking view down the lake to Mount Schoen (1862 m) and its many peaks.

---

81. **Schoen** Lake, Mountain: Named for Otto Schoen, early trapper and expert canoeist.

25.a Schoen Creek Route   Map M25

TRAIL/ROUTE The Schoen Creek route begins at the most southerly campsite on Schoen Lake's west shore. Using caution, cross the Davie River via a secondary logjam, the main one being at the river's exit from the lake. On the south side of the river the hemlock and balsam forest has an imposing primeval quality. Here, the undergrowth is sparse and visibility through the trees is possible for 50m and more. In other spots the trail is overgrown and obscure.

Near the mouth of Schoen Creek, one hour from the campsite and a 10-minute walk from the trail's last brush with the lakeshore, the hiker will reach the end of the defined route and a junction.

To the east the route quickly fades, and to the south is a difficult traverse that heads up the Schoen Creek Valley. The valley route has been used for some years and on the east side of Schoen Creek old step-cut logs provide some brief, relatively easy hiking. From here strong hikers could pick their own route up to a saddle on the south ridge of the mountain. Expect eight hours, round trip, of steady hiking but the difficult trek is well worth the effort.

25.b Nisnak Lake Route   Map M25

ACCESS This route can be reached from Schoen Lake, or from the Upper Adam Road, described later. To reach the east head of Schoen Lake, a 5 km boat trip or paddle is involved, sometimes on rough water. The Nisnak Lake route to the southeast has not been maintained and is overgrown and hard to find. It starts from a natural landing site by a grove of big cedars where there are three camping spots.

TRAIL/ROUTE The route, marked by some old blazes and ribbons, runs through a mature hemlock/spruce forest and is more obvious on the south side of Nisnak Creek. It climbs up on the bench above the creek valley and does not approach the creek until, after two large alder slides— one 200 m wide—it crosses the creek. On the north side of the creek, the route to Nisnak Lake and continuing eastwards has many windfalls and is difficult to locate. Near the lake where a stream enters from the north, there is a single camping spot.

Once through the windfalls the trail meanders through the meadows and isolated stands of timber. Here, it is very well defined and has some muddy and wet parts. From these meadows you can see the five peaks of Mount Schoen and, though too distant to be impressive, Schoen Falls,

Map M25   Schoen Lake Park

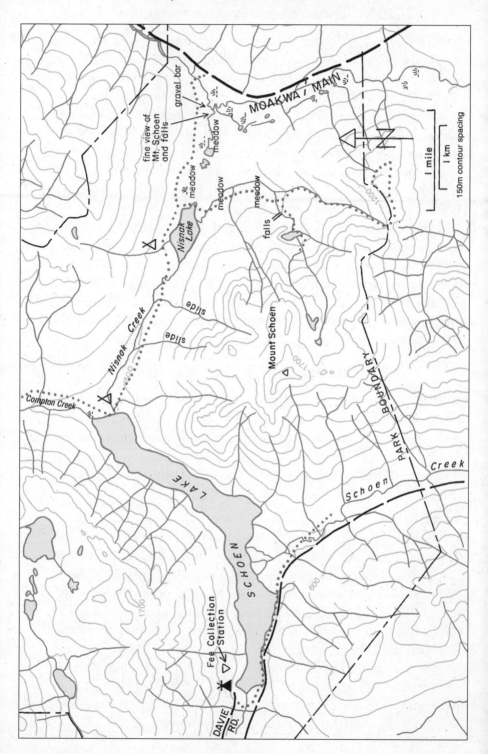

MOAKWA MAIN

fine view of Mt. Schoen and falls

gravel bar

meadow

meadow

meadow

meadow

meadow

Nisnak Lake

falls

Nisnak Creek

slide

slide

Mount Schoen

1700

1200

1600

1 mile
1 km

150m contour spacing

Compton Creek

Schoen Creek

PARK BOUNDARY

SCHOEN   LAKE

1700

600

Fee Collection Station

DAVIE RD.

172

below the fortress-like South Peak. Hiking time from Schoen Lake to Nisnak Meadows is 2 hours, highly dependent upon route-finding, and to the Upper Adam Road, three hours.

ACCESS See maps M25 and M26. The access to Schoen Lake Park from Upper Adam Road is administered by Island Timberlands. There may be active logging in Compton Creek, Adam and Gerald Lake areas. Upper Adam Road is a hauling road, so be aware of heavy industrial traffic. (See Timber Companies, Appendix.)

From the Sayward Junction, drive west on Highway 19 past Keta Lake and a rest area. Just under 10 km from the Sayward Junction, Upper Adam Road parallels and then crosses Highway 19. It is safer to turn right (north) off Highway 19 and take the logging road bridge back across the highway. Follow Upper Adam Road for about 21.5 km to an unsigned parking area on the left.

ROUTES A flagged route (not a trail) goes down to the river from here. Be prepared for wet footing and slippery log crossings. The closest camping spot is a single site on the north side of Nisnak Lake (about an hour.) The Nisnak area is dominated by Mount Schoen with its snowfield and waterfalls. The falls drain into the southeastern corner of Nisnak Lake. Although not on a distinct trail, they can be reached by using the drainage route as a guide and by taking advantage of elk trails and traversing the meadows.

The curved ridge that extends southeast from Mount Schoen can be climbed by following the steep gully that points south above the first falls. On the ridge there is easier walking, probably in snow, and a fine view of Mount Schoen.

Further south along Moakwa Main, you can climb from Gerald Lake to the long ridge extending east from Mount Adam to a subsidiary summit at 1335 m. Allow about one hour to reach the ridge.

The Compton Creek route can be used as a challenging alternative to reaching Schoen Lake. The route is picked up off the end of Compton Creek Main, which is changing with the active logging here. The route was an old trapline that is overgrown and hard to locate on the ground, but there are still some old blazes.

26

Nimpkish Valley

DESCRIPTION There are many hiking, camping, fishing and climbing objectives in the Nimpkish Valley. Access to many of these is dependent upon logging roads. The region is administered by the Regional District of Mount Waddington in Port McNeill.

ACCESS When travelling north there are two routes to the Nimpkish Valley. The most travelled one, from Campbell River and Sayward via Highway 19, is paved all the way and enters the Nimpkish Valley via the Davie River.

The other route is from Gold River on 82 km of unpaved logging roads. From Gold River, Western Forest Products manages the section up to Muchalat Lake and north of Muchalat Lake all the way up to Beaver Cove. From the south, follow the logging roads north from Gold River to either Croman Lake or Woss, where the roads connect with Highway 19. The Croman Lake route via the Klaklakama Lakes is 15 km shorter.

26.a Mount Cain   Map M26

Mount Cain Regional Park, accessed along the road to the campsite at Schoen Lake Provincial Park, Section 25.a, is primarily a ski area but the cut ski routes are hiked in the summer. Seasonal alpine flowers are a delight. This park is also popular with mountain bikers. From the lodge at the bottom of the ski area, about 16 km from Highway 19, you can hike to the ridge west of Mount Cain (1646 m). Expect an elevation gain of about 600 m. The park's spectacular mountain backdrop includes Maquilla Peak, and mounts Cain, Adam and Schoen. For more information contact the Mount Cain Alpine Society at 1-888-688-6622.

26.b Woss Lake Provincial Park Map M26

DESCRIPTION Woss Lake Provincial Park (6634 ha) includes the south end of Woss Lake, its adjacent forests and the permanent snowfields on the northern face of Rugged Mountain, part of the Haithe Range. Rugged Mountain (1875 m), at the head of Woss Lake, is the highest peak in a compact and impressive group of peaks of interest to alpine climbers in both winter and summer.

ACCESS Traditional mountaineering access to this area used to be by water via Woss Lake. Few climbing parties enter this way today. Near Zeballos, WFP logging in the Nomash River Valley to the west of Rugged Mountain has extended roads almost to the south face of Rugged Mountain itself. Current access is via Nomash Main and the unmarked, overgrown and heavily eroded N20 spur near Nathan Creek.

TRAIL A steep hike (through large alder in places) and a scramble from the upper part of this spur will allow hikers to reach the main glacier in 3 or 4 hours. To go farther, experience in glacier travel and rock climbing is required. Carry all climbing gear and beware of avalanches. The Rugged Mountain region is prime black bear habitat. There are no facilities and the park is not patrolled or serviced.

NOTE The Oolichan or Grease Trail was a pre-contact route of native tribes, mainly trading in oolichan oil, a highly prized smelt fish oil. Recently, the Namgis First Nation initiated a process to re-open and utilize the Woss Lake-Tahsis Grease Trail.

This work has included the installation of a composting toilet and shelter at the head of Woss Lake as well as elevated tent platforms in the cedar grove, a tent platform on the saddle at the height of land, and building of three kilometres of trail. A band member, Donald Svanvik, has carved a thunderbird and a wolf in cedar trees at the beginning and along the trail to signify the west coast family ties that the Namgis have with the Mowachaht First Nation. For more details, see Lindsay Elms' website: http://members.shaw.ca/beyondnootka/articles/woss.html

26.c Claude Elliot Provincial Park Map M26

Claude Elliot Provincial Park (289 ha) protects a popular angling lake and its surrounding forest. This area is prime elk and deer habitat. Access is just east of Woss from Highway 19 via North Nimpkish Road and Claude Elliot Main. No camping is allowed.

Map M26 Nimpkish Valley

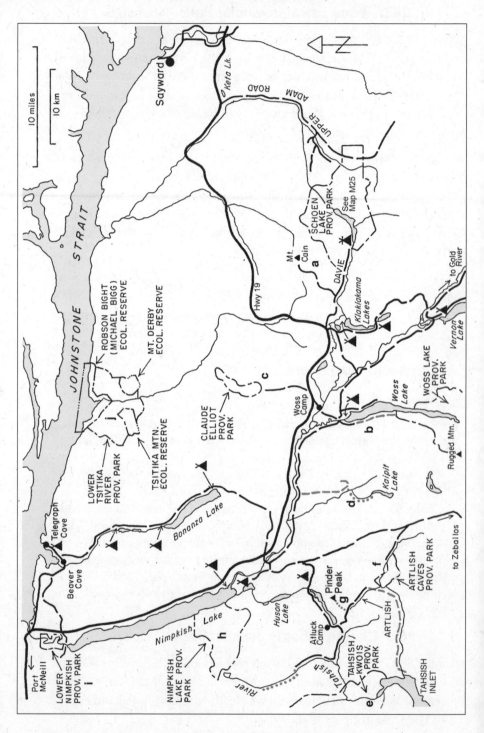

26.d Kaipit Lake Fire Route Map M26

Part of the old fire access trail still exists, but is no longer maintained. This is suitable for strong hikers only. Be prepared for a hefty bushwhack. From Woss Lake recreational campsite, take the logging road to Nimpkish and about 18 km will bring you to the Kaipit turnoff. It is about 7 km to the trailhead where a difficult creek crossing must be made. This heavily overgrown trail, more a route than a trail, passes through beautiful but difficult terrain.

26.e Tahsish Kwois Provincial Park Map M26

The Tahsish River route is obscure and difficult to find, but is accessible at various points along the river from logging roads to the west of Atluck Lake. The trail is prettier upstream.

The Tahsish/Kwois Provincial Park (11,022 ha) includes the Tahsish River Ecological Reserve and the area near the head of Kyuquot Sound's Tahsish Inlet. Access to this remote wilderness is by water from Fair Harbour via Tahsish Inlet, or from the east, down the Tahsish River or by a rugged hiking route along logging roads west of Atluck Lake. Expect heavy logging traffic on these roads. In early 2001, 193 ha were added to the park to preserve the estuary, pockets of old-growth forest and the natural habitat at the mouth of the Tahsish River.

26.f Artlish Caves Provincial Park Map M26

Artlish Caves Provincial Park (254 ha) protects a sensitive area with a future potential as a spelunking destination. Currently, access is extremely difficult and requires travel on logging roads where truck hauling is frequent and a one kilometre hike up a deactivated road near the park's western boundary. A creek crossing en route is susceptible to sudden and dangerous rises in water levels during heavy rains. This region of karst[82] topography is hazardous due to hidden sinkholes and grikes where a hiker could twist an ankle. No camping is permitted.

---

82. **Karst** (from such a region in the former Yugoslavia) refers to an area with underground cavities caused by dissolution of rock. A *grike* is a limestone cleft, widened through solution by carbonation.

26.g Pinder Peak   Map M26

DESCRIPTION Pinder[83] Peak (1542 m), a beautiful headwall south of Atluck Lake, is a rewarding challenge to strong climbers, usually by its southwest ridge, but it is not really a hike.

ACCESS Apollo Road from the south is no longer accessible. Access is off Atluck Main, then up the signed Artlish Main. Drive 4.4 km on Artlish Main, then turn left up a logging spur (not the labelled AR0600.) A high-clearance four wheel drive vehicle is needed. Drive the spur for 2.8 km across many waterbars to a log barrier indicating a bridge out. There is a camping area here at about 600 m elevation.

TRAIL Hike about 30 minutes across two river crossings to the end of the road. This is at [9U647260/5561370NAD83] [9U647265/5561153NAD27]. Hike straight ahead through slash to the old growth timber. Angle left up the creek on its true left side, about 2 hours climbing northeast to a ravine. Climb the gully, then angle right through bush and thick fern to a scree bowl. Climb north, to access the southwest ridge, and continue along the ridge to the summit.

While there is a beautiful view from the ridge, it involves some scrambling in and above the gully, and the upper part is not suitable for hikers.

26.h Nimpkish Lake Provincial Park   Map M26

DESCRIPTION Nimpkish Lake Provincial Park (3950 ha) protects the south end of Nimpkish Lake, the most southerly part of the Karmutzen Range's eastern slopes and most of the Tlakwa Creek drainage, excluding some Crown and privately owned land. Access is by water up Nimpkish Lake starting at the boat launch at the Kim Creek recreation site. This is near the tiny settlement of Nimpkish, off Highway 19 near the southeast corner of the lake. There is rough hiking access via various logging roads. Call the Western Forest Products for updates on road conditions and entry restrictions. (See Timber Companies, Appendix.)

26.i Lower Nimpkish Provincial Park   Map M26

The Lower Nimpkish Provincial Park (265 ha) includes a land corridor on both sides of the Lower Nimpkish River that runs 4 km from Nimpkish Lake's north end. Wherever possible, the corridor is 300 m wide from the

---

83. **Pinder Peak:** Named for William George Pinder (1850-1936), a pioneer land surveyor.

centre of the river, even though the Nimpkish River itself is not part of the park.

Access is via the Nimpkish Heights subdivision, south of Port McNeill, or by foot or water from the north end of Nimpkish Lake. The Nimpkish River can be hazardous. Wilderness camping is allowed. There are no developed trails.

26.j Johnstone Strait Ecological Reserves   Map M26

This is for information only, as no land access to these reserves is available.

Robson Bight (Michael Bigg) Ecological Reserve (5460 ha) is made up of three ecological reserves (Robson Bight, Tsitika Mountain and Mount Derby) and Lower Tsitika River Provincial Park. The reserve was created to provide fragile marine ecosystems in the Robson Bight area. Killer whales use the pebble and smooth rock shores here as rubbing beaches. Whale watching is restricted to Johnstone Strait. The reserve is named after the late Dr. Michael Bigg, a renowned whale researcher.

Merry Widow ridge from north.   TIM SANDER

Port McNeill and Malcolm Island

DESCRIPTION Malcolm Island, just offshore near Port McNeill, was originally settled by Finnish homesteaders at the beginning of the 1900s and the town of Sointula had its centennial in 2002. The community's name is a Finnish word meaning "harmony."

Two great hiking destinations await Malcolm Island visitors, namely the Mateoja Heritage Trail and the Beautiful Bay Trail. Brochures are available locally. For further information contact: Malcolm Island Tourism, Box 217, Sointula, BC, V0N 3E0; or Sointula Resource & Info Centre at (250) 973-2001.

Ferries run between Port McNeill, Malcolm Island and neighbouring Cormorant Island (Alert Bay) about every three hours. Contact BC Ferries at (250) 956-4533 (in Port McNeill), 1-888-223-3779 (toll-free in BC) or www.bcferries.com for schedules.) Sointula's Co-op store and gas station are closed Monday afternoons and all day Sunday.

27a Mateoja Heritage   Map M27

ACCESS On Malcolm Island, from the Sointula ferry dock, take 1st Street to 13th Street and turn right. Turn left onto 3rd Street, continue almost to its end and turn right to the water tower and the Mateoja Heritage trailhead.

TRAIL The 3.2 km Mateoja Heritage Trail (pronounced "Maat te oy a") traverses the site of a 1923 forest fire and passes an historical homestead dating back to the early 1900s. Little Lake has a picnic site and viewing deck. Other highlights are the popular birdwatching area near Melvin's Bog, the small duck pond, and Big Lake, where there is a picnic site, viewing

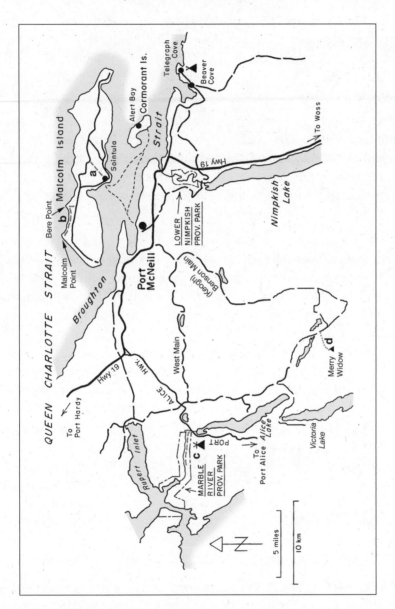

deck and pit toilet. Big Lake is a popular swimming hole. The moderate trail has several benches along the way and ends at the Big Lake Road trailhead. An alternate access to the Big Lake trailhead is via 1st Street, Kaleva Road, Mitchell Bay Road and Big Lake Road. Allow around three hours for a return hike.

27.b Beautiful Bay Map M27

DESCRIPTION This trail runs along the outer side of Malcolm Island. The views are striking on a clear day, including Queen Charlotte Strait and the coastal mountains across the Strait. The Beautiful Bay Trail is rated as moderate with some strenuous sections. The highest point on the trail is 63.7 m.

ACCESS The 5.1 kilometre long Beautiful Bay Trail is located about 6 km from the Sointula ferry dock. Follow 1st Street to Bere Road. Turn right (north) to Pulteney Point Road. Swing left (west) and watch for the Bere Point Campground signs and access road that cuts north to the Beautiful Bay trailhead. Most of the route follows gravel roads. The Bere Point Campground has eight unserviced campsites and a day-use picnic site.

TRAIL From its start at the Bere Point Campground the trail heads north to Bere Point and then turns west along a ridge to parallel Beautiful Bay. Watch for a beach access trail just before the Malcolm Lookout. Next you will pass the Giant Sitka spruce (64.4 m tall). At the trail's mid-point is Puoli Vali Canyon, site of gold panning in the 1930s. Puoli Vali means "halfway along the journey".

The trail drops off the ridge to the beach, on some stairs, and crosses a bridge. It then climbs up Lost Canyon via more stairs back to the ridge and the Numas Lookout, about 3.5 km from the trailhead. More stairs lead down to the beach. Malcolm Point is just over 5 km from the trailhead. At low tide you can loop back to the start along the beach. There have been massive blowdowns due to hurricane force winds, and trees may block the route past Puoli Vali Canyon. Allow one hour to Puoli Vali Canyon; 2.5 hours to Malcolm Point; and five hours for the return trip. Be sure to bring drinking water, as there is none at the campground and none available along the trail.

27.c Marble River   Map M27C (See map M27 for location.)

DESCRIPTION The Marble River Provincial Park trail offers a pleasant 3.7 km walk through mature hemlock/balsam forest, with access to the river. The trail stays on a bench above a shallow canyon cut through the limestone rock by the action of the river. It is a very popular recreation spot, especially for steelhead fishing. Bear Falls is a highlight. Watch for American Dippers cavorting around the falls.

Map M27C Marble River

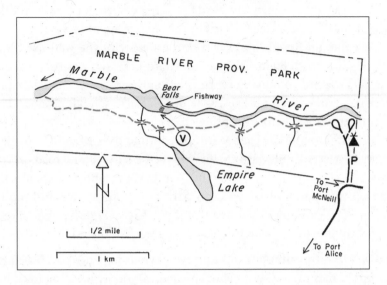

MARBLE RIVER PROV. PARK
Marble
Bear Falls
Fishway
River
Empire Lake
To Port McNeill
P
N
1/2 mile
1 km
To Port Alice

ACCESS From Highway 19, just under 24 km west of the Port McNeill cutoff, take the paved highway towards Port Alice for 14.5 km. Immediately after crossing the Marble River bridge, turn right into a riverside parking area. Leave your vehicle here and walk to the campground and follow the signs to the trail.

TRAIL The trail begins at the river; it takes about two hours to walk to its end. Western Forest Products developed the campsite and trail. In 1995, the provincial government set aside the river canyon area, estuary and adjacent lands at Varney Bay and Quatsino Narrows as Marble River Provincial Park (1512 ha).

27.d Merry Widow Mountain
Map M27D (See map M27 for location.)

DESCRIPTION As one of the northernmost peaks of significant height in the north Island, Merry Widow Mountain (1402 m) is an attractive hiking destination just east of Alice Lake, with views over several large lakes and inlets, mainly to the north and west. You will find lovely meadows and, near the summit, a steep, exposed climb to a prominent viewpoint.

ACCESS Just 2 km west of Port McNeil on Highway 19, turn left onto the Keogh (sometimes called Benson) Main logging road. This turn off is right opposite the road to WFP McNeil office where maps are available, and it is possible to view the world's "largest burl". (There is another "largest" burl in Port McNeil itself by the old elementary school.)

Continue on Keogh Main, left at the fork with the well-used West Main logging road. Follow signs to Maynard Lake and Kathleen Lake for some 30 km until you drive over the Benson River bridge to a T-junction. There is a marked trail for Lac Truite, which is a rough but pleasant 3 km hike on the left just before the bridge.

Turn right onto Alice Lake Main and continue for 1.2 km in a northerly direction. Merry Trail Main (M1080) is the second logging road on your left. Go straight up this, ignoring the spur on your right after about 1 km. Turn up to a point where you can park your vehicle and walk up the long track (5 km) up to the mine site. If you have a high four wheel drive vehicle, you might drive up this very rough track to the mine.

TRAIL From the mine site, hike up the obvious logging road which zig-zags up the mountain side for about 3 km until you see a well-marked trail sign on your right hand side. Hike west up the forested ridge to the open alpine at a peak, elevation 1325 m. The remaining ridge is open alpine, heading southwest to the main peak, which is a short, exposed ridge that non-climbers can ignore.

The Botel Park Trail starts in the tiny North Island community of Winter Harbour. RICHARD BLIER

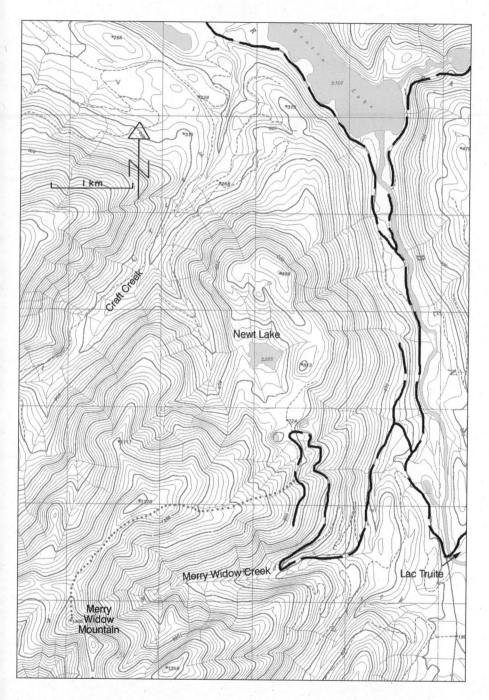

Craft Creek

Newt Lake

Merry Widow Creek

Lac Truite

Merry
Widow
Mountain

1 km

28

Port Hardy, Holberg Area

DESCRIPTION The north and west coasts of Vancouver Island are reached from Port Hardy. Although the mountains as you move north diminish in height compared to Strathcona Park, the Haihte Range, Victoria Peak and Mount Schoen, there is much unexplored wilderness and many unique trails and waterways to entice outdoor adventurers.

LOGGING ROAD ACCESS On all logging roads west of Port Hardy, traffic may be encountered at any time, so watch for loaded logging trucks. Keep your vehicle's headlights on and anticipate meeting a truck at every turn. Western Forest Products logging trucks and vehicles have right-of-way. WFP's Visitor's Guide to Logging Roads and Recreation Areas is a useful adjunct. Copies are usually available at local logging offices in Port McNeill or Holberg and at travel infocentres. This map shows current active logging areas as well as recently built roads and deactivated spurs. This map also details access to Cape Scott, Raft Cove, Grant Bay and over a dozen other major recreation sites. Currently access is open 24 hours a day, but check with WFP's Holberg office for current hauling updates, road conditions and safest travel times.

To reach Cape Scott and Raft Cove provincial parks or Grant Bay and the Winter Harbour area, take the signposted Holberg Road from Highway 19, about 2 km south of Port Hardy. The gravel road from Port Hardy to Holberg (45.5 km) is generally in good to fair condition but the route is narrow and winding.

> **NOTE** Holberg has a gas station (hours of operation vary), a neighbourhood pub and a motel. To get from Holberg to Winter Harbour, West Main and Topknot Main, follow South Main to Winter Harbour (about 25.5 km).

Map M28　Port Hardy Area

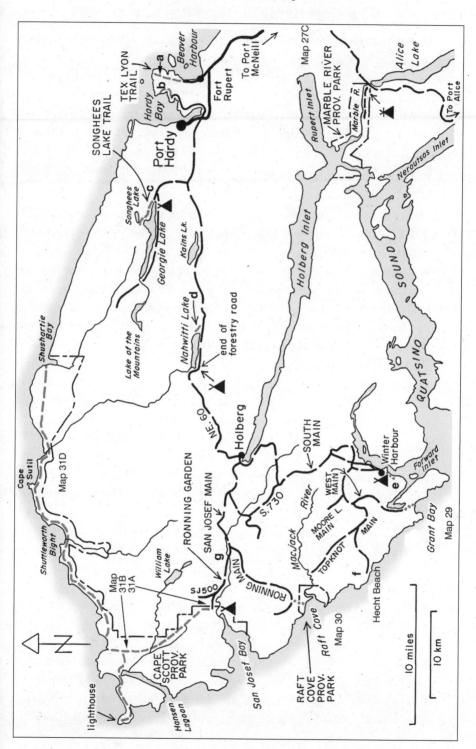

187

28.a Port Hardy to Dillon Point   Map M28A

DESCRIPTION This trail/route starts on a gentle trail from Port Hardy and eventually joins the locally known trail/route, the Tex Lyon Trail, which takes you to Dillon Point. From town, it is about 14 km on the direct route, plus a few side trails.

On the Tex Lyon Trail, especially the last 6 km of this trail, be prepared for a rugged and challenging hike. Basket Eaters' Cove is approximately the halfway point. This is a great destination to view a variety of bird, forest and marine life and the seascapes of Beaver Harbour and Queen Charlotte Strait.

TRAILS From Carrot Park in the town of Port Hardy, follow town sidewalks to the Government Docks, then along the edge of the bay to the Quatse River bridge on Highway 19. There is a large trail map at the east end of the Glen Lyon bridge for the Quatse Loop and the Estuary Trail. At this point you can make a side trip, a 2 km hike from under the bridge up the east side of the Quatse River to Byng Road, over the bridge and back along the west side of the river, first skirting the hatchery, then through the campground, then on the old access gravel road back along the northwest bank.

Continuing on the main trail along the dikes to the Hardy Bay Estuary wildlife viewing area, about 4 km from Carrot Park, head east over the Seven Hills by crossing the BC Ferries road, turn right across the road, walk for 20 m and cross a small footbridge. Climb steadily uphill to a small lake; for about 300 m the trail is on often-slippery logs. After the lake descend about 2 km on a hiking/biking trail to an overgrown logging road that exits near the Fort Rupert school. This is about 8 km from Carrot Park.

It is about 2 km north to the real beginning of the Tex Lyon Trail, which you can reach by walking along either Storey's Beach, opposite the baseball field and BBQ area, or along Storey's Beach Road to the end of Chatham Street in Fort Rupert.

The Tex Lyon Trail is a rugged, 6 km trail to Dillon Point featuring rocky headlands along the shores of historic Beaver Harbour, east of Port Hardy. The trail begins directly over a bridge on Storey's Creek, keeping left at junctions, but it can also be reached past a bluff from the beach at low tides. Watch the tides, as the access at high tide is over a logjam on the creek, above the high tide line. At low tide it is relatively easy to hop across the creek at a narrow spot. For tidal information consult Canadian Tide

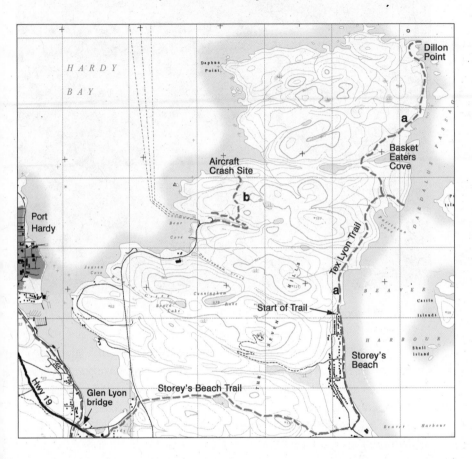

and Current Tables, Vol. 6, available from marine and sporting goods stores. The main trail is above the beach and a rope is in place to assist climbing the steep sections.

There is a viewpoint on the bluff near the start of the trail, with a variety of wildflowers and other plants that grow only in this xeric (dry) microenvironment. Another viewpoint on the north side of Patrician Cove is reached via a brushed-out trail with wooden bridges and a few rope handlines on the steep sections. The viewpoint is about 2.5 km from the trailhead, a good spot for viewing whales, porpoises, seals and a variety of sea birds.

Continue north to a stream descending to Basket Eater Cove, about 1 km further. Turn right at the log bridge. This section includes wet areas and some rotten boardwalks. From the Cove to Dillon Point the 3 km

Natasha Miles on Tex Lyon Trail. TIM SANDER

route follows the beach but sea access is difficult. Ferns and salal tend to overgrow the trail. About 500 m before the Point you have to negotiate a few downed trees. There is an open-sided shelter at the Point, where the view is spectacular.

The last 3 km of this trail is challenging, not suitable for children, dogs, or neophyte hikers. Good boots and long pants are recommended. Take water, food, insect protection, a camera and binoculars to fully enjoy the trip.

The trail is administered through the Regional District of Mount Waddington and the Port Hardy Lions Club. A trail brochure is available and details can be obtained from Development Services at the Regional District of Mount Waddington. (250) 956-3301

28.b Aircraft Crash Site   Map M28A

DESCRIPTION In April 1944 an M117 Dakota overshot the Port Hardy airport, and while repeating its approach it ran out of fuel and crashed just north of Bear Cove near the BC Ferries terminal. Everything of use was salvaged by the army. It is now a National Heritage Site, protected by law.

TRAIL To hike to the site, park at the rest area just before the Ferries terminal. Walk 50 m down the road and turn right uphill on a narrow logging road to a barricade at the gate. Continue up the road on the south side of a valley for about 15 minutes, before doubling back on the north side. Turn right at a stump with survey tapes, about 50 m from the crest of a steep climb, gradually climbing on the narrow path which follows tapes, up a steep slope with several wet patches. The path terminates at the crash site, a good view of Hardy Bay.

28.c Songhees Lake   Map M28

From Highway 19, near Port Hardy, take the Cape Scott/Holberg road and continue about 7 km to the Georgie Lake Forest Service Road. Turn right and follow this seasonally good gravel road another 5 km to Georgie Lake. Loaded logging trucks may use this road. At Georgie Lake there is a sandy beach and a BCFS campground with 5 campsites and pit toilets. The Songhees Lake Trail, an angler's route, leads about 5 km from the campsite to Songhees Lake. The lure is good cutthroat trout fishing. The trail is suitable for all age groups but can be overgrown in spots.

28.d Nahwitti River   Map M28

From Highway 19, near Port Hardy, take the Cape Scott/Holberg road for approximately 24.5 km to the parking area on the right (north) side of the road, just east of Nahwitti Lake. The Nahwitti River Trail winds 2 km alongside the river and through a serene old-growth forest to a tiny pocket beach on Nahwitti Lake.

28.e Botel Park   Map M28

ACCESS Take Holberg Road from Port Hardy to Holberg. From Holberg take South Main a further 25.5 km to Winter Harbour. Winter Harbour is a quaint little fishing village complete with a boardwalk, well-kept old houses, three wharves, a store, restaurant, and a hotel. Just north of the village is the Regional District of Mount Waddington's Kwaksistah seaside campsite guarded by a brightly coloured, eagle-topped totem pole. The Botel Park Trail begins near the end of the road in Winter Harbour.

TRAIL From the small parking area, wooden stairs lead to the trail that meanders through an old-growth forest to a rocky beach on Forward Inlet. Time your hike for lower tides so you can include a beach hike to the southwest. (Use the Canadian Tide and Current Tables: Volume 6.) Hike as far as you can until a jagged headland impedes further progress. Here you will discover a vantage point from which you can gaze down Forward Inlet and the entrance of Quatsino Sound. On a clear day you can make out the distant shape of Brooks Peninsula.

28.f Hecht Beach   Map M28

Take the Holberg Road from Port Hardy to Holberg. From Holberg follow South Main for 22km and turn right on West Main, just north of Winter Harbour. At the West Main/Topknot Main junction, take the right fork. The left fork goes to Grant Bay, see Section 29. Stay on Topknot Main for approximately 11 km, then turn left onto Hecht Main and continue another 5 km to the road end. This secondary road has been deactivated and becomes rough as you approach its end. Watch for the trailhead on the left and the short coastal trail to rugged Hecht Beach.

28.g Ronning Garden   Map M28

DESCRIPTION The Ronning Garden is located on land originally settled by Norwegian Bernt Ronning in 1910. He cleared 2 ha of rainforest and started an exotic garden of imported plants from around the world. The old wagon road from San Josef Bay and the Cape Scott settlement ran by his place and, with an upstairs floor custom-made for dancing and a pump organ below, it is no wonder many travellers made the Ronning homestead a frequent stop. Ronning lived there until the early 1960s.

Many of his plantings still survive, including giant rhododendrons, Japanese cedars, Mexican bamboo and two large monkey puzzle trees that once guarded his long-gone house. The current owners have spent years clearing, restoring and identifying the garden. There is a donation box near the information sign, should you wish to contribute. Contact (250) 288-3724 for details.

ACCESS From Port Hardy take the Cape Scott/Holberg road and head west. Once you reach Holberg, take the San Josef Main, following the signs for Cape Scott Provincial Park. Around 1 km past the Ronning Main/Raft Cove Provincial Park cutoff (left), watch for the Ronning Garden sign and turn right (north) to a small parking area. Turning around here can be a problem so leave room for others. Walk 15 minutes west along the cleared old wagon road to the Ronning Garden.

29

Grant Bay

Map M29; M28 for location

DESCRIPTION Grant Bay is an isolated, but popular, little bay on the north side of the entrance to Quatsino Sound. Bounded by a shoreline of shoals and rock, its main attraction is 800 m of sandy beach. Grant Bay and Browning Inlet are preferred hangouts for bears, but they are unlikely to be a problem as they are genuinely wild and associate people with danger and not with food.

Facing south, Grant Bay is somewhat protected from the open Pacific, and its surf is moderate compared to the exposed west coast beaches. From the beach you can see Cape Parkins, Kwakiutl Point and Cape Cook at the end of Brooks Peninsula. Shore travel and rock scrambling any distance from the Grant Bay beach is difficult; but there is sand and sun and a view of freighters and fish boats passing.

ACCESS From the Highway 19 junction, just south of Port Hardy, take Holberg Road and travel 45.5 km to Holberg. From Holberg, follow South Main, a main haul road, for 22 km and turn right at West Main, just north of Winter Harbour. After travelling about 6 km on West Main, at the junction with Topknot Main, take the left fork and continue south on West Main to cross Kwatleo Creek to its left side. Follow posted signs to the trailhead. WFP has extended West Main south towards Grant Bay. The logging road cuts west (to cross Kwatleo Creek again), then turns south, and eventually runs due east to the new Grant Bay parking area. The Grant Bay Trail was re-established by WFP in the late 1990s.

TRAIL From the parking area it is under half an hour to the smooth sands of Grant Bay. The trail winds southeast through a forest of spruce and hemlock, with very large spruce trees. Sword fern, deer fern and salmonberry are common plants.

Water is available from the stream at the west end of the beach. This is poor-tasting cedar water, but drinkable and should be boiled, filtered or treated. The stream mouth is jammed with sea logs. It is easier to carry extra water in your vehicle. Tents should be placed high on the beach, safely above the high tide mark. There are toilets at either end of the beach.

The trail north from the beach to Browning Inlet, part of the water-access route from Winter Harbour, is lined by thick salal and is usually muddy. It winds through a spike-topped cedar/hemlock forest with scattered large balsams. The route emerges in the southwest corner of the inlet and is marked by plastic jugs in an old fruit tree. This old tree and its neighbours, together with a dike, are the epitaphs to a failed attempt at cultivation. A 50 centimetre high dike extends into the grassy fringe.

Walk north on the relatively firm tidal mud rather than the grassy fringe, which has many small but hazardous natural ditches. You can follow an overgrown route north from the inlet to parallel Kwatleo Creek for about 35 minutes. Encroaching salmonberry crowds the trail near the mouth of the creek. The forest here is spruce and cedar.

There is an alternate access by water. From Winter Harbour launch a small boat, canoe or kayak and head down Forward Inlet, then northwest up Browning Inlet. This is a distance by sea of 9 km. Philip Stooke warns, in his out of print book, *Landmarks and Legends of the North Island*, that at high tide at Quatleyo Point, the tip of the First Nations Reserve, there is an extensive hidden rock ledge which must be avoided. He recommends landing near the north end of the bay. It is best to travel at high tide and be able to get near the Browning Inlet trail. The route from the inlet to the parking area is usually muddy and overgrown with salal. The hike to Grant Bay from Browning Inlet takes just under an hour.

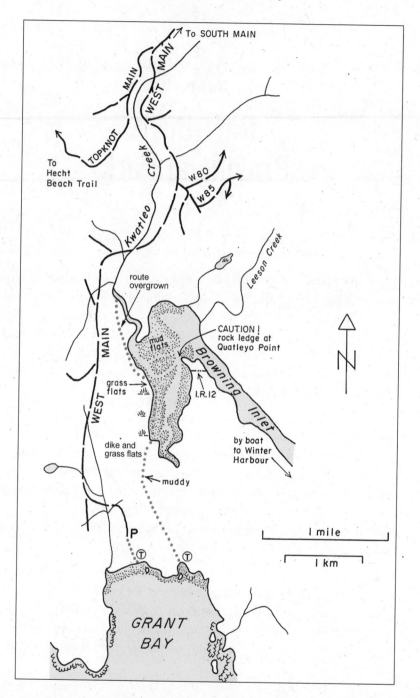

To SOUTH MAIN

MAIN

WEST MAIN

TOPKNOT

To
Hecht
Beach Trail

Kwatleo Creek

W80

W85

Leeson Creek

route
overgrown

mud
flats

CAUTION !
rock ledge at
Quatleyo Point

WEST MAIN

grass
flats

Browning Inlet

I.R.12

dike and
grass flats

by boat
to Winter
Harbour

muddy

P

1 mile

1 km

T

T

GRANT
BAY

30

Raft Cove Provincial Park

Map M30; M28 for location

DESCRIPTION Isolated on the northwest coast of Vancouver Island, south of Cape Scott Park, Raft Cove Provincial Park is distinguished by its 1.3 km length of open sandy beach. The cove offers little protection from the winds and the Pacific surf pounds its shores relentlessly. The Macjack River meanders into the ocean at the south end of the beach. A narrow but forested peninsula separates the Pacific on the west from the Macjack River on the east.

ACCESS To reach Raft Cove Provincial Park, take Holberg Road from Highway 19 near Port Hardy. Travel 45.5 km to Holberg, then continue on San Josef Main and follow the signposts for Raft Cove and Cape Scott provincial parks. A little over 12 km past Holberg on San Josef Main, cut southwest onto Ronning Main, signposted for Raft Cove Provincial Park. After about 10 km from San Josef Main, swing left onto a spur road (Ronning 700). Drive to the end of the secondary road to a limited parking area.

TRAIL The route to Raft Cove takes 45 minutes to hike and begins near the parking area. The rugged route winds about 1.4 km to the beach through mature forests. The first part cuts through WFP forestlands. This route receives minimal maintenance and hikers should exercise care and caution as you will encounter muddy sections and downed trees that you must deal with.

There is possible water access to Raft Cove using canoe or kayak via the Macjack River from the Winter Harbour road systems. Take South Main from Holberg Inlet, turn onto West Main and then onto Topknot

Map M30 Raft Cove Park

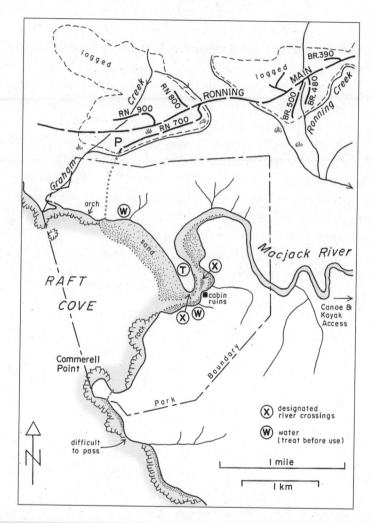

NOTES Summer tenters will enjoy camping on Raft Cove beach. Here there is crashing surf, passing freighters and distant fish boats silhouetted against the horizon. The best water is available from the stream emptying into the south side of the Macjack near the old cabin, although fresh water is also available at the north end of the beach. Remember to boil, treat or filter all cooking and drinking water. There is a food cache approximately at the midpoint of the beach and another closer to the south end. Please use these food caches since bears and other wildlife are common. There is also a pit toilet near the beach's south end.

Main. The short spur road (deactivated) to the Macjack River leaves Topknot Main just under 19 km from Holberg. There is a short 50 m hike to the river. The Macjack is influenced by the tide at this point so plan accordingly, using the Canadian Tide and Current Tables, Vol. 6.

During low tides, shore walks can be made both north and south of Raft Cove. To the south, where small islands of jagged tidal rock stand in sharp contrast to the sands of Raft Cove, an easy 2.2 km walk is possible. South of Commerell Point you will encounter extremely slippery rocks and a steep slope overgrown with salal. Commerell Point itself can be crossed at its neck on a bypass trail.

The cabin on the south side of the Macjack is Willie Hecht's old trapping cabin. It is mouse-ridden and in disrepair. According to L.R. Peterson's *Cape Scott Story*, Hecht and the Boytle family were the pioneers of the Macjack settlement in 1913, but by the early 'twenties only Hecht was left. As early as 1909 a trail had been established from Raft Cove up Ronning Creek to the San Josef Bay/Holberg trail.

31

Cape Scott
Provincial Park

The Cape Scott area is of immense historical interest and the informative, historical interpretive signs at various locations in the park are well worth reading. Opened up by sturdy Danish settlers in the late 1890s, this was the scene of toil and disillusionment. The settlers were gradually defeated in their efforts to homestead the land by the many hardships: the impossibility of getting produce to market, failure of the governments of the day to provide the promised road, stormy winters which made it difficult to land supply boats, cougars which devoured their domestic animals and lack of medical help in emergencies.

But many of the settlers' clearings, roads and buildings are still visible and historically significant. Most homes are now flattened and all equipment has been removed except for the rusting remains of the heaviest implements. The one-time farmlands are deserted. There are countless side trails and old farm sites to discover, as many things as you have time to hunt for. Use caution when exploring these sites; many of the settlers' wells still lie hidden and there may be broken glass and rusty nails scattered about. Old standing structures are unstable.

DESCRIPTION You would need at least a week or more in the area to see everything at Cape Scott Provincial Park (22,131 ha). The whole park is a naturalist's paradise. Most of the trails are the old settlers' roads, some of which were cleared out by the former CFS Holberg Ground Search Team as a 1971-72 Centennial Project. The park was established in 1973. BC Parks' staff does seasonal upgrading.

Cape Scott Provincial Park is a rugged, remote area, where weather can be lovely, or where hurricane-force winds and deluging rains can occur at any time of the year.

Relaxing on Nels Bight, Cape Scott Park. GIL PARKER

Hikers should review all the "Hints and Cautions" at the beginning of this book, (page 12) and in addition should pay particular attention to the following specific points. Hikers should be properly equipped for and familiar with wilderness travel. Gear up for extreme conditions, especially rain and wind.

Secure your vehicle and leave no valuables inside. Parking areas are not patrolled. Respect all private property, First Nations Reserves and historical sites within the Park. Do not remove artifacts. Firearms are prohibited within the Park. Carry NTS topographical maps (1:50,000) 102 I/9 San Josef, 102 I/16 Cape Scott.

Cougars, black bears and wolves inhabit the park's forests and shorelines. Hang your food at night and when you are away from camp. Use the bear-proof food caches where they are provided.

Take your litter out with you and leave nothing to attract bears and small animals. Wash in the ocean, whenever possible, even if you use biodegradable soap. Otherwise stay 30 m away from streams and lakes. If there are no pit toilets dig a hole at least 30 m from lakes and streams. Please ensure that you bury all excrement and toilet paper.

Respect the ocean and know the tidal sequence. Remember that onshore winds can increase a tide height, and of course, so can tsunamis. If you are planning to use the beaches, bring the tide table Canadian Tide and

Current Tables, Vol. 6, published by the Canadian Hydrographic Service.

Random camping is permitted, but BC Parks suggests sticking to established sites, to lessen area impact and prevent the contamination of water sources. Dismantle all temporary shelters completely so there is no trace of them for future visitors. Choose your campsite carefully, to avoid high tides and dangerous trees.

During the summer (June through September) there is an overnight camping fee in place for all backcountry camping in Cape Scott Provincial Park. Help may be available from the Ranger Station at Nels Bight during the summer months. Only in extreme emergency could assistance be forthcoming from the lighthouse. Though you may visit around the lighthouse at Cape Scott, do not expect any hospitality from the staff there.

ACCESS To reach San Josef Bay and the trailhead to Cape Scott, take the Holberg road from approximately 2 km south of Port Hardy and travel 45.5 km to Holberg. Continue on San Josef Main and follow the Cape Scott Provincial Park signposts. The Cape Scott/San Josef Bay trailhead is at the end of San Josef Main, about 18.5 km from Holberg. The entrance to WFP's San Josef campsite is one kilometre before the trailhead. There is parking space at the start of the trail, but on busy weekends vehicles line the roadway.

31.a San Josef Bay to Sea Otter Cove Map M31A

DESCRIPTION A good one-day hike may be made to San Josef Bay and north, as far as Eric Lake. Anyone venturing further in should be properly equipped with backpacking gear and food. About 1 km west of the trailhead the trail forks. To the right (north) is the main Cape Scott Trail and the turn for Eric Lake. To the left is San Josef Bay, about a kilometre, and its beautiful wildlife marshes and expanses of sandy beaches. Most of the trail to San Josef is surfaced with gravel, well graded and wheelchair accessible.

WATER ACCESS You can canoe or kayak down the San Josef River all the way to the surf at San Josef Bay. You need favourable sea and wind conditions and, because the river is affected by tides, you have to be precise in calculating river tides. A good flood tide eliminates many of the rapids and shallows that develop on an ebb tide. Be ready to portage and line. Put in at the WFP campsite or from the BC Parks boat launch. The latter is reached at San Josef Heritage Park, at the end of the spur

Map M31A   Cape Scott (South)

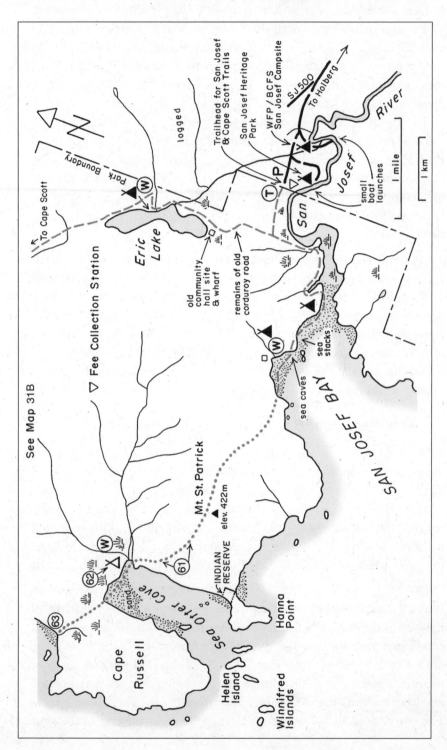

To Cape Scott

Park Boundary

logged

Trailhead for San Josef & Cape Scott Trails

San Josef Heritage Park

WFP / BCFS San Josef Campsite

SJ 500

To Holberg

San Josef River

1 mile

1 km

small boat launches

Eric Lake

old community hall site & wharf

remains of old corduroy road

▽ Fee Collection Station

See Map 31B

sea stacks

sea caves

SAN JOSEF BAY

Mt. St. Patrick
elev. 422m

INDIAN RESERVE

61

62

63

sand plain

Sea Otter Cove

Hanna Point

Cape Russell

Helen Island

Winnifred Islands

N

202

road, halfway between the WFP campsite and the Cape Scott/San Josef Bay trailhead. Both of these water access points are suitable for canoes and small cartop boats.

TRAIL At the far end of San Josef Bay, a rough route climbs to the top of Mount St. Patrick (422 m), which affords a magnificent viewpoint. The summit is covered with crowberry. On the trail there are sections which are swampy and some which are steep.⑥¹ From the summit the trail leads to Sea Otter Cove, approximately 10 km from the trailhead. Currently this trail has had little if any work done on it, except for the occasional clearing of windfalls. Faded markers can be found on some trees. Fresh water is present at the cove, but you must bushwhack up the creek about 100 m to be above the tides. The route around the head of Sea Otter Cove is passable only at mid to low tide. Camping ⑥² in the bush above the cove is marginal and the grasses are awash at high tide. From here it is about 2 km to Lowrie Bay ⑥³ where you will find large burls in the forest, fresh water and high-tide beach camping. Anyone contemplating this rugged route should carry the topographical map and a compass.

31.b San Josef River to Nissen Bight
Map M31B (also map M31A)

DESCRIPTION The Cape Scott Trail, now 23.6 km long, follows the settlers' trails and an old telegraph line that ran from Holberg Inlet northwest to Fisherman Bay, Hansen Lagoon and the Cape Scott lighthouse. The old telegraph wire can still be seen in some locations.

TRAIL The first part of the trail is in the Quatsino Rain Forest, where between 380 cm and 510 cm of rain falls annually, so here the trail is always muddy. From the San Josef Bay Trail junction, hike north on the main Cape Scott Trail to the first campsite from the trailhead, at Eric Lake. BC Parks has installed 13 tent pads, fire rings, food caches and a pit toilet. This is a scenic treasure, with warm swimming and cutthroat trout fishing only metres away on the gravel bar at the mouth of the creek running into Eric Lake.

Fisherman River, 9.3 km from the trailhead, has a good bridge, but you should be careful at some of the other creek crossings. There is water at Donaldson's Farm.⑥⁴ Near the junction to the old townsite, a grave off-trail on the right marks the Christiansen boy's grave.⑥⁵ Farther on you come to the sign-posted turn-off to Hansen Lagoon and Nels Bight.

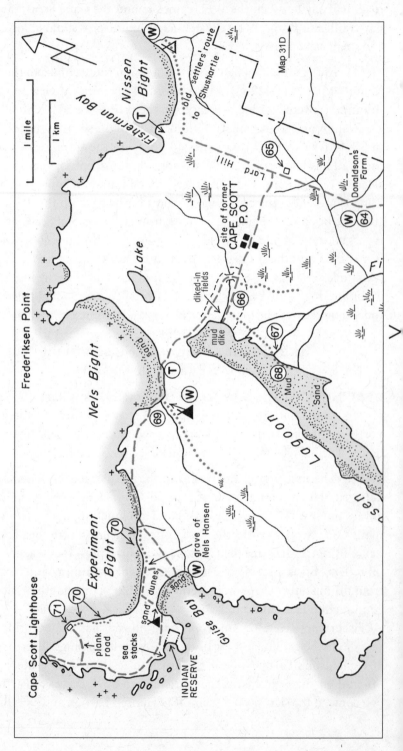

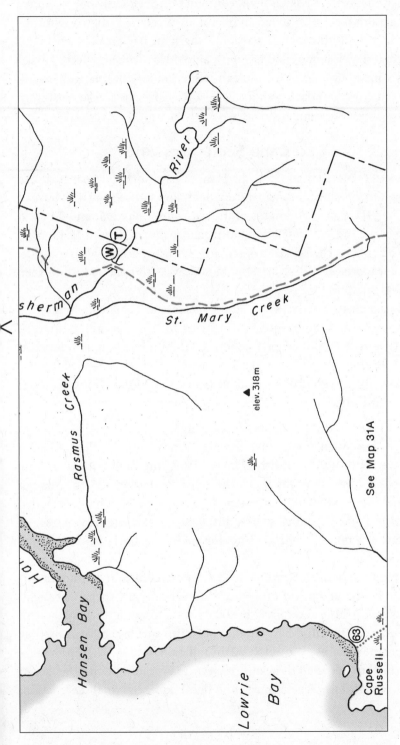

River

sherman

St. Mary Creek

Rasmus Creek

W T

▲ elev. 318m

See Map 31A

Hansen Bay

Lowrie Bay

Cape Russell

63

ID H

The trail north to Nissen Bight continues through fairly open country of sphagnum bogs with cedar and hemlock vegetation, then down slippery "Lard Hill" through timber to Fisherman Bay and Nissen Bight. Fisherman Bay is a gravelled bay with an old wooden shipwreck. Nissen Bight is made up of 800 m of clean white sand, with relatively small, evergreen growth to the foreshore. The North Coast Trail heads east from Nissen Bay. (See Section 31.d.)

31.c Cape Scott   Map M31B

DESCRIPTION Returning to the Hansen Lagoon/Nels Bight turn-off, hike west to the site of the former Cape Scott Post Office and farm, burned down in 1971, past the remains of the old community hall and down to the several hundred hectares of flat meadowland at Hansen Lagoon.(66) Remnants of breached dikes still remain, past a log bridge (67) at low tide. These meadows were diked (68) by the settlers with rock and fill to keep out the tidal waters.

The lagoon, part of the Pacific Flyway, is a seasonal habitat for migrating Canada geese and other waterfowl. During the summer, the salt marsh flats at Hansen Lagoon offer a good growth of goose tongue (plantain) grass. Look for the succulent "sea asparagus" which, when added to soup and stews, forms a good dietary supplement to freeze-dried food. Salmonberries, huckleberries and salal berries are plentiful in summer.

TRAIL To get to the big surf beach, Nels Bight, take the trail to the right at the BC Parks sign as you reach the lagoon meadow. Nels Bight, 16.8 km from the trailhead, has nearly 2 km of flat white sand with pounding surf. At the west end of the beach there is a good water supply although BC Parks advises that all park water should be treated, filtered or boiled before use. Pit toilets have also been installed at two locations as shown on our map. The ranger cabin (69) is not for public use, but is a seasonal base for park rangers.

From Nels Bight the trail to the lighthouse climbs in behind an impassable headland (70) and drops back to the beach at Experiment Bight, with its sandy shore and rolling breakers. Walk through thick salal on an old plank road to Guise Bay, another beautiful surf beach. At Guise Bay there are the remains of an old RCAF installation from W.W.II. From there go north through sand dunes to the jeep road leading uphill for about 2 km through lush vegetation to the lighthouse, the final destination.

Read the notice board at the lighthouse. The Cape Scott lighthouse was built in 1960 and is still staffed.

On returning to Guise Bay, walk across the sand dunes back to the northern shore, and return to Experiment Bight along the beach past lovely little rocky coves, to make your hike at the Cape into a round trip. Hanging floats mark headland bypass routes.

Optionally, by going down the plank side road to the supply landing ⑦1 and out to the end of the longest guy wire, you can find a primitive trail to the beach and thus, return to the sand neck by beaches and headland by-pass trails. Be alert for black bears.

HISTORY Once you could hike farther, out to the very tip of Vancouver Island. First you went through the gate, near the lighthouse, and down a series of seemingly endless steps and wooden staircases. Next you crossed a couple of jagged tidal rock cuts on two swaying cable suspension bridges. Another stretch of wooden boardwalk extended to the Cape Scott foghorn. From just beyond here, you could shelter from the almost-incessant winds and watch the waters beneath you churn and roil, as angry seas challenged defiant headlands. What was a spectacular highlight of any journey to Cape Scott is now a part of history. The trail, stairs, boardwalk and two lofty suspension bridges were closed by the federal government and removed in 1999.

31.d Nissen Bight to Shushartie Bay   Map M31D

DESCRIPTION The new North Coast Trail was opened in 2008 in the Nahwitti/Shushartie addition to Cape Scott Park along remnants of the old Shushartie route. This trail is very beautiful and remote, a combination of overland routes, headlands and beach walking. It is quite challenging with many steep headland trails and difficult cobble and boulder beaches. There are several developed boardwalks to cross extremely wet boggy areas.

As with the adjacent Cape Scott Park, this new addition has many historical sites, including the locations of important native settlements on the north coast.

ACCESS The west end of the trail is 15.3 km from the San Josef trailhead. North Island Transportation, (250) 949-6300, will transport to or from Port Hardy and the trailhead parking lot; their scheduled runs are Tuesday and Thursday.

Map M31D   North Coast Trail

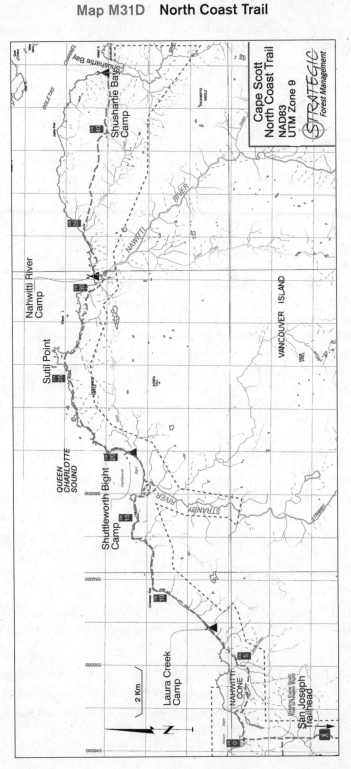

Current access to the east end is still uncertain; road access is very difficult, but water access is available to the trailhead on the west side of Shushartie Bay. Water taxi service from Port Hardy is provided:

- Cape Scott Water Taxi: 1-800-246-0093 or (250) 949-6541
  www.capescottwatertaxi.ca
- Catala Charters: 1-800-515-5511 or (250) 902-1031
  www.porthardywatertaxi.net

TRAIL It is a 43 km trek from Nissen Bight to Shushartie Bay. The route includes 18 km of beach hiking, 25 km of inland trails, 2263 metres of boardwalk and 822 metres of stairs. Two cable cars cross the Strandby and Nahwitti rivers. Developed campsites (tent pads, toilets, food caches) are located at Laura Creek, Irony Creek (Cape Sutil) and Nahwitti River. There is also a campsite at Skinner Creek (Shushartie Bay.) The first official party required 5 days to complete the 43 km .

NOTES Hikers should be totally self-sufficient for any kind of emergencies. Some sort of communication device is recommended; cell phones may not function here.

Leave a planned schedule with a responsible party. Tide tables and the ability to read and understand them are critical. Be aware of the possibility of surge tides and (hopefully rare) tsunamis. Review the Hints and Cautions section at the beginning of this book and Section 31.

A brochure describing the North Coast Trail is planned but not available at time of publication. A waterproof version of a map similar to ours is available in some outdoors stores. Contact also Strategic Forest Management Inc., Port McNeill, B.C., Tel: (250) 956-2260.

Contact B.C. Parks for information. The only trail references at this time are on the Northern Vancouver Island Trails Society website: http://www.northernvancouverislandtrailssociety.com

At website www.wildcoastmagazine.com there is an article and a downloadable trail description.

APPENDIX

Vancouver Island Trails Information Society

The Vancouver Island Trails Information Society (VITIS) is a non-profit society dedicated to providing accurate information to the public about parks and trails on Vancouver Island. The object of the society is to increase the interest of the general public in the outdoors and in hiking, by publishing information relating to these activities.

The first edition of *Hiking Trails I, Victoria and Vicinity,* was published in 1972, followed by *Hiking Trails II, Southeastern Vancouver Island* in 1973 and *Hiking Trails III, North Vancouver Island, including Strathcona Park* in 1975. Originally the society was formed as the Outdoor Club of Victoria Trails Information Society under the direction and leadership of Editor, Jane Waddell Renaud. In 1993, to eliminate confusion, the society changed its name to the Vancouver Island Trails Information Society. Our society has an unbroken 35-year history of producing hiking trails books covering all of Vancouver Island. We also maintain an up-to-date web site with additional support and resource information. VITIS members are Eric Burkle, Irm Houle, Betty Burroughs, Joyce Folbigg, Grahame Ruxton and John W.E. Harris. These volunteer members maintain the operation of the society and guide the production of the Hiking Trails books.

Information is gathered with the assistance of dedicated hikers and climbers who have contributed accurate descriptions of trail conditions, suggested corrections and pointed the way to new hiking destination. We would also like to thank the many individuals, organizations and agencies noted in the Recognition of Contributors Section who have provided helpful information.

For more information about VITIS
e-mail: trails@hikingtrailsbooks.com or visit
website: www.hikingtrailsbooks.com
telephone: 250-474-5043 or toll free 1-866-598-0003
fax: 250-474-4577 or toll free 1-888-258-4213

VITIS has confidence in the reliability of information about the hiking trails and backcountry routes presented in this volume as of publication date. However, the pace and scope of change makes uncertain the information regarding management agencies, organizational arrangement, the provision of services and maintenance of facilities. Any guidebook provides a snapshot of the terrain and the trails at a given point in time. Readers must be aware that there are regular changes in organizational structures, roles and capabilities of BC Parks and BC Forest Service, and of the ownership and tenure operation of various lands by timber companies.

This is important for access issues, but also, a greater reliance on 'no trace' camping practices and 'self maintenance' of the land is needed.

Hikers are encouraged to check with the contacts suggested in the book before venturing where there are uncertainties. *Hikers are also encouraged to check our website for changes, and to report any discrepancies that they know about. See above website and E-mail address.*

Reader Survey

We are always striving to improve our hiking books. In order to continue to produce the kind of book you want, we would like to get a better understanding of our readers. As well, we would also like your suggestions on how future editions can be improved in order to continue our successful 35-year history of publishing these books on a non-profit basis.

Thank you for your participation in this survey. In recognition of how important this is to us, we will periodically select a name from the responses received. The 'winner' will receive a current edition of *Hiking Trails* of their choice. Please note that all responses are treated in confidence and that your e-mail address will not be shared with others. To participate in the survey, please go to our website at: www. hikingtrailsbooks.com/survey

Abbreviations
(see also Club Addresses and Timber Companies)

BCFS	British Columbia Forest Service	SAR	Search and Rescue
		SPPAC	Strathcona Park Public Advisory Committee
FOSP	Friends of Strathcona Park		
FSR	Forest Service Road	SWI	Strathcona Wilderness Institute
GPS	Global Positioning System		
NAD	North American Datum (In Canada, based on 1927 or 1983)	TCA	Tourism, Culture and the Arts
		UTM	Universal Transverse Mercator

Club Addresses

Alberni Valley Outdoor Club
(AVOC)
www.albernivalleyoutdoorclub.org

Alpine Club of Canada (ACC),
Vancouver Island Section.
http://accvi.ca

Comox District Mountaineering
Club (CDMC)
www.comoxhiking.com

Heathens Mountaineering Club
(Campbell River)
www.heathensweb.ca

Island Mountain Ramblers (IMR)
(Nanaimo)
http://islandmountainramblers.
blogspot.com/

Outdoor Club of Victoria (OCV)
www.ocv.ca

Victoria Club Tread
www.clubtread.org

Many of these clubs may be contacted
through:

The Federation of Mountain Clubs
of BC (FMCBC)
130 West Broadway, Vancouver, BC
V5Y 1P3
Tel. (604) 873-6096
e-mail: fmcbc@mountainclubs.bc.ca
www.mountainclubs.org

The Outdoor Recreation Council
of BC
334 - 1367 West Broadway,
Vancouver, BC V6H M20B9
Tel. (604) 737-3058
e-mail: outdoorrec@orcbc.ca
www.orcbc.ca

Map Sources

Some logging company recreation
maps are available. Check with local
offices (see Timber Companies, page
215) and tourist infocentres.

Some Search and Rescue organizations publish area recreation and
logging road guides including:

Maps of the Comox Valley,
published by
Comox Valley Ground Search
and Rescue Association
PO Box 3511, Courtenay, BC V9N 6Z8
(co-sponsored by the Comox
Valley Chamber of Commerce);
comoxvalleysar@yahoo.ca

Campbell River Area Logging Road
and Backcountry Map: Published by
Campbell River Search and Rescue
Society, PO Box 705, Campbell River,
BC, V9W 6J3.

Sold at most outdoor and hunting
stores, some gas stations, etc. North
Island Logging Road and Backcountry
Map also available, as of 2008.

Mussio Ventures' Backroad
Mapbook for Vancouver Island
Enquire at 1-877-520-5670 or
(604) 438-3474
www.backroadmapbooks.com

Geological Survey Canada
101 – 605 Robson St., Vancouver, BC
V6B 5J3 (604) 666-0271

International Travel Maps
and Books
530 West Broadway
Vancouver, BC V5Z 1E9
(604) 879-3621

Island Blue Print,
905 Fort St., Victoria, BC
V8V 3K3 (250) 385-9786
1-800-661-3332 (toll-free)

Mountain Meadows
Sporting Goods
368 Fifth St., Courtenay, BC
V9N 1K1
(250) 338-8732
1-866-882-8885 (toll-free)

Nanaimo Maps and Charts
8 Church St., Nanaimo, BC
V9R 5H4
1-800-665-2513 (toll-free)

Robinson's Sporting Goods
1307 Broad St., Victoria, BC
V8W 2A8
(250) 385-3429

Spinners Stores
Discovery Harbour Mall
164 - 1436 Island Highway
Campbell River, BC V9W 8C9
(250) 286-6166
1-888-306-4444 (toll-free)

Clover Point Cartographics
152 Dallas Road, Victoria, BC
V8V 1A3
(250) 384-3537
1:20,000 for B.C. and
specialized maps
www.canadamapstore.com

Crown Publications Inc.
106 Ontario Street
Victoria, BC V8V 1M9
www.crownpub.bc.ca
(250) 386-4636

Provincial Park and other specialized
maps are available from **Canadian**
Cartographics in Port Coquitlam, BC
1-877-524-3337.

These and aerial photos can be
ordered from:

Administrative Officer/
Air Photo & Lab Services
(250) 952-4050
http://www.basemaps.gov.bc.ca/

Useful References

Toll-free calling to provincial government offices is available through:

Enquiry BC
(250) 387-6121 or (outside Victoria/
within BC) 1-800 663-7867.

BC Ferries   For route and
reservation information call
(250) 386-3431 (in Victoria, or long
distance from outside North America),
or 1-888-BCFERRY
(1-888-223-3779)
(anywhere in North America)
fax (250) 381-5452 or visit:
www.bcferries.com

Ministry of Forests and Range
For BCFS information visit the
following website: www.gov.bc.ca/for/

Trails and related issues are now part
of the Ministry of Tourism, below.

Port McNeill Forest District
PO Box 7000, Port McNeill, BC
V0N 2R0
(250) 956-5000

Campbell River Forest District
(250) 286-9300. Same address as
Tourism, Culture and the Arts,
next page.

Ministry of Tourism, Culture and the Arts

http://www.tsa.gov.bc.ca/sites_trails/
Under this site you may explore the Documents and Forms Library, including the Recreation Manual (dealing with management of a wide range of recreational activities) and a List of Recreation Sites.

Please note that every community has a "Visitor Information Centre."

Discovery Coast District
(Campbell River – North Island)
Charlie Cornfield, Recreation Officer
370 S. Dogwood Street
Campbell River, BC V9W 6Y7
Phone: (250) 286-9422 or
general number (250) 286-9300

BC Parks
For information on provincial parks, visit the BC Parks, Ministry of Environment, website at
http://www.env.gov.bc.ca/bcparks/
BC Parks, Ministry of Environment
PO Box 9398 Stn Prov Govt
4th floor, 2975 Jutland Road
Victoria BC V8W 9M9

NVI Mining
(formerly Boliden/Westmin)
Myra Falls Operation, PO Box 8000,
Campbell River, BC V9W 5E2
(250) 287-9271
(There is a first-aid kiosk in the parking lot, where an emergency phone might be available. There is a pay phone in the recreation building.)

City of Campbell River
Parks, Recreation and Culture
301 St. Ann's Rd.
Campbell River, BC V9W 4C7
(250) 923-7911

Regional District of Comox/ Strathcona
350–17th Street, Courtenay
BC V9N 1Y4
(250) 334-6000
www.rdcs.bc.ca

Regional District of Mount Waddington
PO Box 729, Port McNeill, BC
V0N 2R0
(250) 956-3301
www.rdmw.bc.ca

Port McNeill Tourist Information Centre
(250) 956-3131

National Hiking Trail (Hike BC)
All over Canada, work is proceeding on the National Hiking Trail that will stretch coast to coast across the country. In a few regions this hiking only corridor will follow the same route as the Trans Canada Trail, in others it will be a separate hiking alternative. Planning for a potential route in the north part of Vancouver Island continues. For current information contact:
http://www.nationaltrail.ca/
Hike%20BC.htm

Trans Canada Trail (Trails BC)
The Trans Canada Trail is a multi-use trail that extends from Atlantic to Pacific and even to the Arctic Ocean, although in many places it is still in process of development. On Vancouver Island, the trail runs from Victoria to Nanaimo via Lake Cowichan, then connects to the mainland via ferry.
http://www.trailsbc.ca

Search and Rescue

Call 911

Call out for search and rescue emergencies is done via telephoning 911. The local Search and Rescue organizations will only respond through the "lead organizations," namely the RCMP and BC Ambulance. The Joint Rescue Coordination Centre (military) is involved in air and marine rescue, again through the RCMP. While no phone numbers are given to avoid unfiltered call outs, the following organizations deserve your support, donations of funds or volunteer assistance:

Alberni Valley Search and Rescue

Arrrowsmith Search and Rescue (Qualicum Beach)
kenneden@telus.net

Campbell River Search and Rescue
PO Box 705, Campbell River,
BC V9W 6J3.

Comox Valley Ground Search and Rescue
Box 3511, Courtenay
BC V9N 5N5
comoxvalleysar@yahoo.ca

North Island Search and Rescue
Port Alice, V0N 2N0

Port McNeill Search and Rescue
V0N 2R0

Sayward Search and Rescue
V0P 1R0

Timber Companies

Western Forest Products
Regional Office in Port McNeill
(250) 956-4446
Port McNeill Division
Holberg Division
Englewood Division (Woss)
Jeune Landing Division (Port Alice)

TimberWest
General Enquiries
(250) 729-3700
North Island Division
Campbell River
(250) 287-9181

Island Timberlands
For all I.T. areas call
(250) 755-3500
in their Nanaimo office.
Eve River, Kelsey Bay and
Menzies Divisions
Northwest Bay Division
Port McNeill Timberlands
Sproat Lake Operation

Strathcona Wilderness Institute (SWI)

SWI is a non-profit society, which, through public education, promotes an appreciation and awareness of the natural world – particularly in and around Strathcona Provincial Park on Vancouver Island. SWI operates under a cooperative agreement with BC Parks. The Institute's year-round public education program includes lectures, exhibitions, special events, research projects and publications, as well as educational courses such as Wilderness Self-Reliance, Medicinal Plants, Geology in Strathcona Park, Fall Birding and Coast to Coast Treks.

Interest in creating a Wilderness Institute resulted from a 1992 conference at Strathcona Park Lodge, organized by the FOSP and attended by representatives from forestry, tourism, education and parks sectors. The conference focused on society's relationship to wilderness. What emerged was a resolve to protect existing wilderness areas, along with some methods by which this could be achieved. Based on an agreement that society in general needs to be more knowledgeable about, and more in contact with, the natural world, the Strathcona Wilderness Institute was formed in 1994.

Parts of Strathcona Provincial Park are Important Bird Areas (IBAs), designated sites which provide essential habitat for breeding and non-breeding White-tailed Ptarmigans. Vancouver Island's ptarmigans are a subspecies (Lagopus leucurus saxatili) found nowhere else in the world.

Sighting cards will be made available at selected trailheads. If you spot a White-tailed Ptarmigan, contact Dr. Kathy Martin, Department of Forest Sciences, UBC, Vancouver, BC V6T 1Z4. (Use the cards if possible.) For more information call the Strathcona Wilderness Institute at (250) 337-1871. SWI and FOSP: Box 3404 Courtenay, BC V9N 5N5.

Friends of Strathcona Park (FOSP)

FOSP is a non-profit society with an interest in Strathcona Provincial Park. Stewardship of the park is the key objective of The Friends, and they actively support the management directives described by Strathcona Park's Master Plan. Current activities centre on supporting proposed additions to Strathcona Park, and include discussions with forest industry companies that own land on the park's boundaries. The Friends also sponsor trail-building projects, and have formally "adopted" the Bedwell River Trail.

Strathcona Park Lodge

Located on the eastern shore of Upper Campbell Lake, 41 km west of Campbell River on Highway 28 to Gold River and 6 km before the road enters Strathcona Provincial Park, this internationally known outdoor recreation centre is well-situated for visitors to this part of the park.

The Lodge offers quality meals and accommodation, and a year-round program for all ages. Instructional courses range from nature walks and canoe camping to white-water kayaking, rock climbing and west coast explorations. The latter include guided hikes along the Nootka Trail. For more information and a free brochure contact: Strathcona Park Lodge, PO Box 2160, Campbell River, BC V9W 5C5 (250) 286-3122 or visit http://www.strathcona.bc.ca

Strathcona Park Public Advisory Committee (SPPAC)

The Strathcona Park Public Advisory Committee (SPPAC) meets at least twice a year to provide the Environmental Stewardship Regional Manager with advice and strategies for managing Strathcona and Strathcona-Westmin provincial parks. SPPAC (created in 1994) has been very successful and has been used as a model for other provincial advisory groups.

Varied issues include the implementation of the Master Plan and annual modifications, permit applications, public concerns, dwindling provincial funding and specific items referred by the Regional Manager, his staff or the Committee.

Committee members (up to 11 people) possess a broad range of interests, knowledge and expertise that includes a solid understanding of topics relating to Strathcona Provincial Park, aboriginal culture, geology, outdoor recreation, resource management and conservation.

The public are invited to attend SPPAC meetings, which are advertised in local newspapers.

Recognition of Contributors

Although Hiking Trails 3 covers all of Vancouver Island north of Parksville, Qualicum, and Port Alberni, for years the heart of the book has been the trails and routes of Strathcona Provincial Park, which itself covers over 250,000 ha. Our thanks go out once again to the principal contributors to the original version of this book: John S.T. Gibson, Dan Hicks, Ruth Masters, Jack Shark and Syd Watts; to the three previous editors, Jane Waddell, James Rutter and Richard Blier; and to the many others who contributed to the original compilation in 1975 and to subsequent revisions.

Throughout the years and the book's various editions, dedicated hikers and climbers have contributed accurate descriptions of trail conditions, offered detailed trip accounts, suggested corrections, and pointed the way to new hiking destinations. The 10th Edition of Hiking Trails 3 is no exception. Many people went out of their way to ensure that map and text queries were answered correctly. Their efforts are appreciated.

Special thanks go to the following who have provided key assistance for this edition: Barb Baker, Lindsay Elms, Glenn Lewis, Ron Quilter, Cheryl Noble, Darryn McConkey, Shawn Hedges, Peter Rothermel, Steve Smith, Doug Cowell, Craig Wagnell, Sandy Briggs, Martin Smith, Fraser Harris, Jerry Davidson, Tim Sander, Judy and Richard Leicester, Don Cameron, Rick Eppler, Aldyth Hunter, Rick Hudson, Tony and Anita Vaughn, Bill West-Sells, Al Huddlestan, Jonathon Lok, Brad Sedola, Brian Allaert, Ron Lepine, Gordon Welsh, Cathy Denham, and Steven Rogers.

For valuable assistance and information we thank: BC Forest Service, BC Parks, Ministry of Environment, Ministry of Tourism, Culture and the Arts, TimberWest, Western Forest Products, Island Timberlands, Regional District of Mount Waddington, Regional District of Comox Strathcona, Strategic Forest Management Inc., Federation of Mountain Clubs of BC.

Thanks also to Frances Hunter of Beacon Hill Communications Group, book designer, and Jim Bisakowski of Desktop Publishing Ltd., map designer, for their friendly, cooperative approach to completing Hiking Trails 3.

Gil Parker, Editor

Suggested Reading

(A random selection, some out of print, but in libraries)

Akrigg, G.P.V. and Helen B. *British Columbia Place Names.* Vancouver: UBC Press, (3rd ed.), 1997.

Alberni Environmental Coalition. *Alberni Valley Trail Guide.* Port Alberni: 2006.

Baikie, Wallace. *Strathcona: a history of British Columbia's first Provincial Park.* Campbell River: Ptarmigan Press, 1986.

Baron, Nancy and Acorn, John. *Birds of Coastal British Columbia.* Vancouver: Lone Pine Publishing, 1997.

Blier, Richard K. *More Island Adventures: An Outdoors Guide to Vancouver Island.* Victoria: Orca Book Publishers, 1993.

Blier, Richard K. *Island Backroads: Hiking, Camping and Paddling on Vancouver Island.* Victoria: Orca Book Publishers, 1998.

Blier, Richard K. (ed.) *Hiking Trails I: Victoria & Vicinity.* Victoria: Vancouver Island Trails Information Society, (13th ed.), 2007.

Blier, Richard K. (ed.) *Hiking Trails II: South-Central Vancouver Island and the Gulf Islands.* Victoria: Vancouver Island Trails Information Society, (8th ed.), 2000.

Colbeck, Lynda A. *Vancouver Island Shores.* Nanaimo: Transcontinental Printing Inc., 1998.

Donaldson-Yarmey, Joan. *Backroads of Vancouver Island and the Gulf Islands.* Vancouver: Lone Pine Publishing, 1998.

Elms, Lindsay. *Beyond Nootka: A Historical Perspective of Vancouver Island Mountains,* Courtenay: Misthorn Press, 1996.

Goldberg, Kim. *Where To See Wildlife on Vancouver Island.* Madiera Park: Harbour Publishing, 1997.

Guppy, Walter. *Wilderness Wandering on Vancouver Island,* 1993.

Hayman, John. *Robert Brown and the Vancouver Island Exploring Expedition.* Vancouver: University of British Columbia Press, 1991.

Horvath, Pal. *The Nootka Trail: A Backpacker's Guide.* (Self-published)

Jones, Laurie. *Nootka Sound Explored: A Westcoast History.* Campbell River: Ptarmigan Press, 1991.

Kahn, Charles. *Hiking the Gulf Islands.* Victoria: Orca Book Publishers, 1995.

Lebrecht, Sue and Susan Noppe. *Adventuring Around Vancouver Island.* Vancouver/Toronto: Greystone Books, 1997.

McKnight, George. *Sawlogs on Steel Rails.* Port Alberni: Port Alberni Seniors' History Committee, 1995.

Parker, Gil. *Aware of the Mountain, Mountaineering as Yoga.* Victoria: Trafford Publishing, 2001.

Parker, Gil. *Coast Mountain Men, Mountaineering Stories from the West Coast.* Victoria: Aware Publishing, 2007.

Payne, David. *Island Cycling: A Cycle Camper's Guide to Vancouver Island.* Victoria: Orca Book Publishers, 1996.

Petersen, Lester R. *The Cape Scott Story.* Langley: Sunfire, 1985.

Pojar, Jim and Andy Mackinnon. *Plants of Coastal British Columbia.* Vancouver: Lone Pine Publishing, 1994.

Scott, Christine. *Nature Campbell River.* Courtenay: ABC Printing, 2001.

Smith, Ian. *The Unknown Island.* Vancouver: Douglas & McIntyre, 1973.

Stoltmann, Randy. *Hiking the Ancient Forests of British Columbia and Washington.* Vancouver/Edmonton: Lone Pine Publishing, 1996.

Stone, Philip. *Island Alpine: A Guide to the Mountains of Strathcona Park and Vancouver Island.* Heriot Bay: Wild Isle Publications, 2003.

Taylor, Jeanette and Douglas, Ian. *Exploring Quadra Island: Heritage Sites & Hiking Trails.* Quathiaski Cove: Fernbank Publishing, 2001.

Walbran, John T. *British Columbia Coast Names.* Vancouver: Douglas & McIntyre, 1971.

Wild, Paula. *Sointula: Island Utopia.* Madiera Park: Harbour Publishing, 1995.

Wood, Rob. *Towards the Unknown Mountains.* Campbell River: Ptarmigan Press, 1991.

See also:
http://www.comoxhiking.com/local-history.htm for Forbidden Plateau and Strathcona Park place names.

Index

About the Editor

Gil Parker is a structural engineer who worked for Dominion Bridge and for Willis, Cunliffe, Tait & Co. He created a solar energy firm, Ark Solar Products Ltd., later consulting on solar energy in Saudi Arabia and India. Through Dalvos Pacific Trading, Gil managed a trading and agency representation in Eastern Russia.

Gil is a life member of the Alpine Club of Canada and has climbed in Canada, the United States (including Alaska), Russia, Georgia, India and Nepal. He has hiked extensively in the Grand Canyon and throughout the southwest States, Copper Canyon in Mexico, Patagonia in Argentina and Chile, and has completed most of the Pacific Crest Trail from Mexico to Canada.

As a freelance writer, Gil has specialized in articles on outdoor adventure, conservation, the environment and international issues. Gil is past-president of the Victoria School of Writing. His books are:

Bridging the Pacific　　　*Aware of the Mountain*
Looking through 'Glasnost'　　*Mom, Marian & Me*
Coast Mountain Men

Gil has held executive positions in the Alpine Club of Canada, the World Federalists of Canada, the Solar Energy Society, Victoria School of Writing, the Victoria-Khabarovsk Association and the Sister City Advisory of Victoria. He is an Honorary Citizen of Victoria. For work in developing Rotary in Russia, the Rotary Club of Victoria-Harbourside awarded him a Paul Harris Fellowship. He holds a Distinguished Service Award from the Alpine Club of Canada.

Also in this series:

Hiking Trails I
Victoria & Vicinity

Hiking Trails II
South-Central
Vancouver Island
and the Gulf Islands

*Published by Vancouver
Island Trails Information
Society and distributed
by Orca Book Publishers*

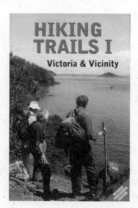

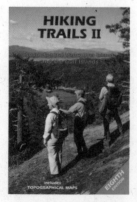